Maths
made easy

Rajesh Kumar Thakur currently works as a Director at the National Vedic Maths Academy, a branch of the All India Ramanujan Maths Club, Gujarat. He is a postgraduate in three diverse subjects—Mathematics, Operational Research and Education and has done his Doctorate in Education on Vedic mathematics. He has been teaching secondary and senior secondary school students for the past 14 years and has written more than 30 books and around 100 mathematical articles and dozens of research papers in national and international journals. To popularize Vedic Mathematics, he has thus far conducted more than 250 seminars in different states in India and trained more than 50000 students. He has also conducted several talks as well as the National Level Math Quiz show on All India Radio. He loves writing poetry and has written many poems, dozens of which have been published in various magazines of repute. Mr Thakur has received many awards, including the National Best Teacher Award by AIRMC in 2010. In the year 2014, the All India Ramanujan Maths Club honoured him with a Special Achievement Award for conducting 125 free workshops on mathematics in the year 2012.

Also by the author:

The Essentials of Vedic Mathematics
Mathematics in Religion

Maths
made easy

Rajesh Kumar Thakur

RUPA

Dedicated to my son Nilabh Thakur
And my niece Nitya Thakur

Published by
Rupa Publications India Pvt. Ltd. 2015
7/16, Ansari Road, Daryaganj
New Delhi 110002

Sales centres:
Allahabad Bengaluru Chennai
Hyderabad Jaipur Kathmandu
Kolkata Mumbai

Copyright © Rajesh Kumar Thakur 2015

While every effort has been made to verify the
authenticity of the information contained in this book,
the publisher and the author are in no way liable for the use of the
information contained in this book.

All rights reserved.
No part of this publication may be reproduced, transmitted,
or stored in a retrieval system, in any form or by any means,
electronic, mechanical, photocopying, recording or otherwise,
without the prior permission of the publisher.

ISBN: 978-81-291-3679-4

Fifth impression 2017

10 9 8 7 6 5

The moral right of the author has been asserted.

Printed at Shree Maitrey Printech Pvt. Ltd., Noida

This book is sold subject to the condition that it shall not, by
way of trade or otherwise, be lent, resold, hired out, or otherwise
circulated, without the publisher's prior consent, in any form of binding
or cover other than that in which it is published.

Contents

Preface   *vii*

1. Addition Is Fun — 1
2. Subtraction in Seconds — 12
3. Multiplication Is Easy — 20
4. Multiplication Without Paper — 54
5. Division Without Dilemma — 74
6. Square: Child's Play — 84
7. A Special Method for Square — 95
8. Square Root Is Not Tough — 110
9. Cube: A Piece of Cake — 120
10. Cube Root in a Playful Manner — 126
11. Finding Percentage in your Head — 139
12. Doing Fractions Is so Much Fun — 150
13. Trigonometry Is No More Tiring — 171
14. Conversion Made Easy — 194

Bibliography — 199

Preface

Mathematics was called the queen of all subjects but nowadays a stigma has been attached to it. Recent surveys on the status of mathematics in Indian schools have revealed the truth that mathematics is really one of the most dreaded subjects amongst students. If you look at the findings of the NCERT and private agency ASER you will be surprised to know that more than 50 per cent of students of class 5 can't recognize numbers and can't do simple subtraction and division. Former Prime Minister Dr Manmohan Singh declared the year 2012 as National Mathematics Year to celebrate the 125th birth year of the renowned mathematician Ramanujan. It was then that I wondered if there is an urgency behind the declaration by the Government of India in declaring the year as National Mathematics Year. I then decided to devote a whole year to trace the cause of the backwardness of our students in mathematics. In that process I travelled to different parts of India and gave 125 lectures in different schools and colleges and tried to reason out the backwardness of mathematics in India. The conclusion which I drew from my 125 marathon lectures in the following two months was that it was the calculation part which students hated the most. Now the question is who is the real culprit in such a scenario? In my opinion the design of the curriculum of mathematics has made the subject very insipid. Mathematics is one of the most interesting subjects in the whole universe if taught in the right way. Very few students now love mathematics and those who love this subject know how faithful and fruitful this subject is.

I have made a small effort to resolve the problem regarding the calculation part to boost the morale of students to take up this subject seriously, as mathematics is the soul of all subjects. In the present book, I have extensively used the finger technique for multiplication and in trigonometry too I have tried to use the finger technique to find the value of different angles of trigonometric ratios. Moreover, in subtraction I have tried to use the simplest method which is effective in all conditions, saves time and avoids any confusion. The methods for multiplication, square, cube, fraction and many more have been discussed in very simple language in the chapters.

Like my previous book *The Essentials of Vedic Mathematics*, which reveals the Vedic technique of solving arithmetical problems as well as algebraic problems in no time, this book also reduces the calculation time making it very effective. The language of the book is so simple that even a layman can understand it properly and get mastery over his calculations.

This book in its present format could not have been possible without the guidance of Mr Kapish Mehra, the managing director of Rupa Publications, who took the initiative and made me write a book which will not only help students to do calculations in no time but will also consolidate the foundational stone of mathematics and make mathematics a fun subject. I am thankful to my wife Namita who allowed me to use the pictures of her hand gestures in this book to make it look as if someone is presenting the demo live.

My sincere thanks goes to Ms Ruchi Nagpure, (Asst Prof., CIT Raipur) and my friend Mr Amit Chandan for their support in writing this book.

Lastly, I would request my avid reader to evaluate my work by giving me their valuable suggestions to improve the quality of the book. For any suggestions or errors that may have occurred in this book feel free to email me. This will help me to improve this book in the next edition.

Rajesh Kumar Thakur
E-mail: rkthakur1974@gmail.com

1

Addition Is Fun

Addition is one of the most common mathematical operations, which even a layman uses frequently. Whether you go for shopping or purchasing your grocery, books, or other daily used commodities you need to calculate your expenditure and here the addition technique comes handy.

Have you ever visited a bank? I'm sure you have. Now my question is—how does the cashier add the cashbook account so fast? The answer is very simple, he uses some tricks or adopts some methods which comes with practice and develops a method of his own to calculate fast.

You must have noticed the greengrocer mentally adding the cost of objects purchased. A more astonishing fact, which you will not believe is that some of them haven't been to school but are equally efficient at calculations.

In my book, *The Essentials of Vedic Mathematics*, I have focused on the Vedic technique and discussed the various methods which are better than the conventional method taught in schools, but here I shall focus on some of the unconventional methods and tricks which will help you calculate faster than the method you use and many a times you will see that you can compete with a calculator.

Addition of 5 Consecutive Numbers

Addition of 5 consecutive numbers can be done by various

methods but the simplest one is to multiply the highest number by 5 and subtract 10 from the result obtained.

Example:– 13 + 14 + 15 + 16 + 17 =?

Solution:– Here the highest number is 17
Multiply it by 5: 17 × 5 = 85
Subtract 10: 85 – 10 = 75

Example:– 66 + 67 + 68 + 69 + 70 =?

Solution:– Here the highest number is 70
Multiply it by 5: 70 × 5 = 350
Subtract 10: 350 – 10 = 340

Now the question you may ask: If there are more consecutive numbers then what strategy shall you use to find the total?

I am giving here some points and expect you to generalize a rule to add consecutive numbers on your own.

- If there are 4 consecutive numbers; multiply the highest by 4 and subtract 6 (1½ × 4)
- If there are 5 consecutive numbers; multiply the highest by 5 and subtract 10 (2 × 5)
- If there are 6 consecutive numbers; multiply the highest by 6 and subtract 15 (2½ × 6)
- If there are 7 consecutive numbers; multiply the highest by 7 and subtract 21 (3 × 7)
- If there are 8 consecutive numbers; multiply the highest by 8 and subtract 28 (3½ × 8)

You can add consecutive numbers more smartly if you understand the two cases.

Case 1:– If there are odd numbers of consecutive terms.
Rule:– Multiply the middle term by the number of terms.

Example:– 12 + 13 + 14 + 15 + 16 + 17 + 18 + 19 + 20

Solution:- Since there are 9 terms so the middle term = 16
Multiply it by 9 = 16 × 9 = 144

Case 2:- If there are even numbers of consecutive terms.
Rule:- Take the mean of the two middle terms and multiply it with the number of terms.

Example:- 23 + 24 + 25 + 26 + 27 + 28 + 29 + 30 = ?

Solution:- You can see that there are 8 consecutive numbers to be added. The two middle numbers are obviously 26 and 27
Take the mean of the two = 26.5
Multiply it with the number of terms = 26.5 × 8 = 212
I am hopeful that you would have generalized the rule to add the consecutive numbers. Leave this apart and learn some interesting methods to add fast.

Addition of Two Numbers in Case One of the Numbers Ends With Repeated 9s or 8s

You can add two numbers in your mind without doing much effort from your side if you see one of them has repeated 9s or 8s.

Example:- a) 98765 + 999 = ?
b) 78976 + 9998 = ?

Rule:- Round off one of the number into multiple of 10s and do the balancing act.

Solution:-

$$= 98765 + 999$$
$$-1| \quad |+1$$
$$= 98764 \quad 1000$$
$$= 98764 + 1000 = 99764$$

Example:- 78976 + 9998 = ?

Addition is Fun 3

Solution:–
```
78976 + 9998
 –2|        |+2
78974    10000
= 78974 + 10000 = 88974
```

Addition of Similar Digits Repeated

Addition of similar digits with digits repeated in ascending order sometimes creates problem as you have to arrange them according to their place value before adding. Let me simplify this problem to make such addition a child's play.

Example:– $5 + 55 + 555 = ?$

Rule:– a) Take the digit repeated and replace all the repeated digits with 1
b) Count number of digits in each number.
c) Multiply the result 123... by the repeated digit.

Solution:– a) Take 5 common and replace all 5 with 1
$5 (1 + 11 + 111)$
b) Count number of digits in each number. Here the digit 1 has been repeated 1, 2 and 3 times.
c) Multiply 123 by 5

Hence, $5 + 55 + 555 = 5 \times 123 = 615$

Example:– $5 + 55 + 555 + 5555 + 55555 = ?$

Solution:– a) Take 5 common and replace all 5 with 1
$5 (1 + 11 + 111 + 1111 + 11111)$
b) Count number of digits in each number. Here the digit 1 has been repeated 1, 2, 3, 4 and 5 times.
c) Multiply 12345 by 5

Hence, $5 + 55 + 555 + 5555 + 55555 = 5 \times 12345 = 61725$

Example:– $9 + 99 + 999 + 9999 + 99999 + 999999 = ?$

Solution:– a) Take 9 common and replace all 9 with 1

$$9 (1 + 11 + 111 + 1111 + 11111 + 111111)$$

b) Count number of digits in each number. Here the digit 1 has been repeated 1, 2, 3, 4, 5 and 6 times.
c) Multiply 123456 by 9

Hence, 9 + 99 + 999 + 9999 + 99999 + 999999 = 9 × 123456 = 1111104

Addition of Repeated Digits with Decimals

Addition of repeated digits after the decimal can be done easily in the same manner as discussed above with the only difference that here the counting of numbers will be in the reverse order.

Example:– 0.9 + 0.99 + 0.999 + 0.9999 =?

Solution:– Here the repeated digits are in ascending order. The number of 9s after decimal parts are 1, 2, 3 and 4. Reverse the order of repetition and multiply it by the repeated digit 9
Hence, 0.9 + 0.99 + 0.999 + 0.9999 = 9 × 0.4321 = 3.8889

Example:– 0.7 + 0.77 + 0.777 + 0.7777 + 0.77777 + 0. 777777 =?

Solution:– Here the repeated digits are in ascending order. The number of 7s after decimal parts are 1, 2, 3, 4, 5 and 6. Reverse the order of repetition and multiply it by the repeated digit 7
Hence, 0.7 + 0.77 + 0.777 + 0.7777 + 0.77777 + 0.777777 = 7 × 0.654321 = 4.580247

Example:– 0.4 + 0.44 + 0.444 + 0.4444 + 0.44444 + 0. 444444 +0.4444444 + 0.44444444 = ?

Solution:– Here the repeated digits are in ascending order. The number of 4s after decimal parts are 1, 2, 3, 4, 5, 6, 7 and 8. Reverse the order of repetition and multiply it by the repeated digit 4

Hence,
0.4 + 0.44 + 0.444 + 0.4444 + 0.44444 + 0.444444
+0.4444444 + 0.44444444 = 4 × 0.87654321 = 3.50617284

Addition of Repeated Digits in the Whole and Decimal Parts Together

So far we have seen two cases. In the first one we only dealt with whole numbers and in the second case we dealt with decimal fractions. In the third case we will deal with both the cases together. Let's learn the rule.

Rule:– a) Calculate the decimal part and do as done in case 1
 b) Calculate the whole part.
 c) Add both the results and you will get the answer.

Example:– 3.3 + 3.33 + 3.333 + 3.3333 = ?

Solution:– a) In the second case we learned how to deal with numbers with only decimal parts.
 0.3 + 0.33 + 0.333 + 0.3333 = 3 × 0.4321 = 1.2963
 b) Here the number 3 in the whole part is repeated 4 times; i.e. 3 × 4 = 12
 c) Add both the parts

Hence, 3.3 + 3.33 + 3.333 + 3.3333 = 12 + 1.2963 = 13.2963.

I hope you have enjoyed the magic of addition a lot. Let's practise this before I move on to the next method for addition.

a) 45 + 46 + 47 + 48 + 49 + 50 = ?
b) 78 + 79 + 80 + 81 + 82 = ?
c) 2.2 + 2.22 + 2.222 + 2.2222 + 2.22222 = ?
d) 0.6 + 0.66 + 0.666 + 0.6666 = ?

Faster Addition in the Group of 10

Have you ever tried to discover the reason behind your mistake in adding large numbers? If I am not wrong then it is the carry-over problem. Adding larger numbers in a length takes a lot of time as we are not accustomed to adding larger numbers.

$5 + 3 + 2 + 8 = 18$ is right but $9 + 8 + 7 + 9 + 6 + 8 + 8 + 5 + 9 + 7 + 4 + 9 = ?$ is difficult to answer. So what I have done here is to break the sum in different parts for convenience. In simple words, whenever the sum of digits exceeds 10, we put a dot over the digit in the preceding column and take the unit digit to add to the next number and the process keeps continuing. It is important to understand here that the dot marks on any digit placed has the value 1 more than itself.

I.e. $\dot{9} = 10$

Example:—

```
      3 2 9 7 3 6
       . .   .
        4 6 5 7 2 8
     . .   . . .
      0 6 2 3 9 9 9
       .
    +   5 5 4 3 2 1
      1 9 7 3 7 8 4
```

Explanation: Addition for each column will be done as you generally do in the normal addition. For the convenience of readers the arrow has been shown moving downwards.

In the first column:

- $6 + 8 = 14 > 10$ so place a dot over $\dot{2}$, the number preceding 8. Take the excess 4 ($14 - 10 = 4$) to the next number of 1st column.
- $4 + 9 = 13 > 10$ so place a dot over 9, number preceding 9 of the first column and take the excess 3 ($13 - 10 =$

Addition is Fun 7

3) to the next number of the 1st column.
- 3 + 1 = 4 since there is no more digits left in the first column so final sum 4 should be written in the bottom line.

In the second column:

- 3 + $\dot{2}$ (=3) + $\dot{9}$ (=10) = 16 > 10 so place a dot over 9 in the third column and take the excess 6 (16 – 10 = 6) to the next number of the second column.
- 6 + 2 = 8. Since there is no more digits left in the second column so the final sum of the second column is written below the line.

The sum of the rest of the columns will be done accordingly.

Now you may ask a question:– What if the sum of digits is more than 10 and there is no column left?

The answer is very simple—put a zero behind the number in the preceding column.

In the sixth column 3 + 4 + 6 = 14 >10, so a dot needs to be put to the preceding number in the seventh column hence a zero (**0**) is placed in the seventh column.

Let us take another example to understand the whole process of addition

Example: 124 + 4234 + 8238+ 646 + 5321 + 3510 + 8989 =?

Solution:

```
              1 2 4
          4 2 3 4
        0̄ 8 2 3̄ 8
          0̄ 6̄ 4̄ 6
          5 3 2 1
        0̄ 3 5 1 0
        0̄ 8̄ 9̄ 8̄ 9
      + 3 1 0 6 2
```

Explanation:–

In the first column:

- $4 + 4 + 8 = 16$. It is more than 10, so a dot is placed next to 8 i.e. on 3. Here dot on 3 makes it one richer by itself.
  $\bar{3} = 3 + 1 = 4$
- Take the excess 6 (16-10 = 6) and move to the next digit. The sum of $6 + 6 = 12 > 10$. So place a dot on 4, next to 6 in the preceding column.
- Again 2(excess of the previous stage) + 1 + 0 + 9 = 12 so placing a dot on 8 write the final 2 at the end of first column.

In the second column:

- $2 + 3 + \dot{3}(= 4) + \dot{4}(= 5) = 14$ is more than 10, so dot is placed to the preceding number 6 in the third column.
- Proceed with the excess $14 - 10 = 4$ and add the remaining digits in the second column.
  $4 + 2 + 1 + \dot{8}(=9) = 16$
- Write the excess 6 (16-10) below the second column and move to the third column likewise.

This process will be continued till every column is taken into account. Once you practise the example shown in the first method, it will be easier for you to understand the second example and do some fast calculation.

Now this is the time for practising some problems.

	1.		2.		3.	
		587		2568		2654793
		256		9856		6501547
		875		8555		8725780
		250		7426		3571598
		569		7840		1729617
	+	253	+	3654	+	6540

Addition is Fun

Hope you have enjoyed this method too. Before I wind up this chapter let me show another interesting method to you. This method simply works on manipulation of numbers and breaking them.

Let's see the breaking up of numbers in terms of 10s to add conveniently.

Example:– 26 + 59 + 394 + 66 + 11 + 14 = ?

Solution:–

Step 1:– Here, the complete observation shows us that 26 + 14 are likely to yield a rounded result. The same would be the case if 59 and 11 were paired. Moreover, the pair 394 and 66 yield a rounded result.

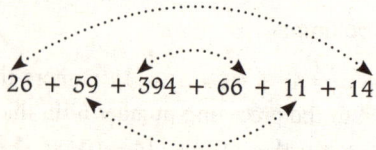

Step 2:– Rearrange the pair and add as per the pairing done above.

= (26 + 14) + (59 + 11) + (394 + 66)
= 40 + 70 + 460
= (40 + 460) + 70
= 500 + 70
= 570

Addition by Double Column Method

In the double column method we break up the numbers to be added in columns, taking two numbers in each columns.

Suppose you have to add 2345 + 5768 + 8764 + 9127, we will break these numbers into two parts and keep adding two numbers by breaking in the multiples of ten so that we can do addition conveniently.

$2+23+50+7=82$
$82+87=80+80+9=169$
$169+91=169+1+90=260$

```
  2
 23   45
 57   68
 87   64
+91   27
───   ──
260   04
```

$45+68=40+60+5+8=113$
$113+64=110+60+7=177$
$177+20+3+4=204$

Now you can invent your own rule to club the numbers according to your choice in any order by considering the fact that you have to make multiples of 10 to add smoothly. The above examples will help you invent your own rule to add numbers.

Addition is Fun

2

Subtraction in Seconds

Introduction

For most of us the name given to this chapter will not sound awesome. You may think that the name of this chapter should have been 'Subtraction is Troublesome'. Subtraction is merely the other side of the coin of addition. Let me first address your concern. Why do we find subtraction to be a boring topic? I do hope the given example will tell you the actual truth behind our genuine fear.

Example:– Subtract 4768 from 8436

Solution:–

```
       7 13
       ̷8 12
         ̷2 16
     ̷8 ̷4 ̷3 ̷6
   – 4  7  6  8
   ─────────────
     3  6  6  8
```

The above example is an eye-opener for all of us. So many operations performed to get a simple answer may sometimes annoy us and deter us from doing subtraction in our heads.

Why Is Subtraction Tough to Handle?

There are probably two reasons for this.

   a) While many of us learned our addition tables by heart

in school, few of us really mastered the conversion of these into subtraction tables with anything approaching the same thoroughness.

b) Borrowing is regarded to be the main problem as far as subtraction is concerned. The traditional method of borrowing is tricky and many of us find ourselves forgetting to borrow, or borrowing twice.

I shall try to address both of your concerns in this chapter and I will prove that once you complete this chapter you will say—hurray, subtraction is so easy!

Mathematical Terms in Subtraction

```
  9 2 7 8    Minuend
- 3 0 4 1    Subtrahend
  -------
  6 2 3 7    Remainder
```

Complement method

We shall now use the complement method to do subtraction which will become an easy addition. The complement of a number is the difference of that number from base 10. I have placed two hands together to show you the complement of each number which you can use initially to understand the modus operandi. This device can be used to teach students this new technique. This is so simple that even a grade 3 student will rejoice in doing subtraction by this method.

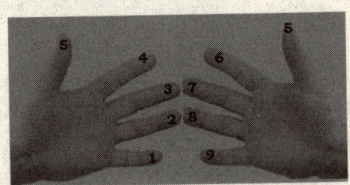

Figure 2.1: *Picture showing complement of each number*

Warm-up Round for Mental Subtraction

To subtract mentally, try and round off the number you are subtracting and then correct the answer.

- To subtract 9 subtract 10 which is quite easy and add 1.
- To subtract 8 subtract 10 and add 2.
- To subtract 7 subtract 10 and add 3, etc.

Example:– 56 – 9 = ?

Solution:– In order to avoid carry; take 10 from 56 in your head which is a simple act and then add 1.

$$56 - 10 = 46 \qquad 46 + 1 = 47$$

Example:– 64 – 7 = ?

Solution:– Take 10 from 64 in your head which is a simple act and then add 3.

$$64 - 10 = 54 \qquad 54 + 3 = 57$$

Example:– 84 – 39 = ?

Solution:– First round of the number 39 into 40 and add 1 in order to adjust it. The whole operation can be done mentally.

$$84 - 40 = 44 \qquad 44 + 1 = 45$$

Example:– 567 – 87 = ?

Solution:– First round of the number 87 into 100 and add 13 in order to adjust it. The whole operation can be done mentally.

$$567 - 100 = 467 \qquad 467 + 13 = 480$$

Don't worry, these are warm-up exercises, which show that you can do simple subtraction mentally by manipulating the question according to your own ease. Let me play another warm-up game before I put my focus on your actual trouble. Wait, the climax is still a mile away!

Subtraction from a Power of 10

Start moving from right to left. Replace every zero from the left with a 9 and the last zero with a 10. The extreme left digit before zero will get reduced by 1. Now do the simple subtracting without worrying about mistakes.

Example:– 10000 − 462 = ?

Solution:–
```
   10000        will       9 9 9 10
 −   462      become      −  4 6 2
                           9 5 3 8
```

Example:– 40000 − 1172 = ?

Solution:–
```
   40000        will       3 9 9 9 10
 −  1172      become      − 1 1 7 2
                           3 8 8 2 8
```

Here, the extreme left digit i.e. 4, will get diminished by 1, and all the zeros thereafter will change into 9, except the last one. The last zero on the extreme right will be changed to 10.

Example:– 50000 − 27172 = ?

Solution:–
```
   50000        will       4 9 9 9 10
 − 27172      become      − 2 7 1 7 2
                           2 2 8 2 8
```

Here, the extreme left digit 5 will get diminished by 1, and all the zeros thereafter will change into 9, except the last one. The last zero on the extreme right will be changed to 10. The whole operation can now be done mentally in no time.

Here Comes the Method Which You Were Awaiting Eagerly

Warning   **Warning**   **Warning**

Before I proceed further I would like to remind you one thing which is very important to mention here that if you haven't read the examples before and are directly jumping over to the new method STOP and GO BACK to the previous examples and see the operation and understand the method and come back. I hope you will not do any cheating this time and follow my advice wisely. You may ask me a question:

How Will This Method Help You Do Subtraction Faster?

- This will enable you to work from left to right. Though initially you will find it uneasy to work with, but mind you this method works better from left to right as against the traditional method which works from right to left.
- This technique will help you tackle any **borrowing**.
- The most annoying part of subtraction comes when you are asked to subtract a larger number from a smaller one—the process that causes so much confusion and error.

How Does This Method Operate?

- Start subtracting from left to right.
- In case you have to subtract a larger number from a smaller number just take the complement of the larger number to be subtracted and add it to the smaller number. While doing so, reduce the previous digit of answer by 1.

Example:– 34 – 27 = ?

Solution:–
```
   3 4
 - 2 7
 ─────
   ̸1 7
```

We first put 1 down as 3 – 2 = 1. Now move to the second digit from left. Here you are in a critical situation where you need the help of complement method.

4 – 7 = 4 + complement of 7 = 4 + 3 because 7 > 4

16 *Maths Made Easy*

Since we used the complement for the second digit from left so 1 written at the first place will be reduced by 1.

Example:– 534 − 287 = ?

Solution:–
```
    5  3  4
 −  2  8  7
   2̸3̸4̸5̸7
  = 2  4  7
```

5 − 2 = 3   3 − 8 = 3 + 2 (Complement of 8) = 5   4 − 7 = 4 + 3 (Complement of 7) = 7

Every time we use the complement its previous digit gets reduced by 1. For 3 − 8; we reduce the previous digit 3 by 1 and write 2 in its place. For the next subtraction 4 − 7; we reduce the previous digit 5 by 1 and write 4 at its place as shown above.

Hence, 534 − 287 = 247

Example:– 54386 − 32458 = ?

Solution:–
```
    5  4  3  8  6
 −  3  2  4  5  8
   2 1̸ 2̸ 9 2̸ 3̸ 8
  = 2 1 9 2 8
```

5 − 3 = 2
4 − 2 = 2̸ = 1 (since complement in the next digit is used so 2 is finally reduced by 1; 2 − 1 = 1)
3 − 4 = 3 + 6 (Complement of 4) = 9
8 − 5 = 3̸ = 2 (since complement in the next digit is used so 3 is finally reduced by 1; 3 − 1 = 2)
6 − 8 = 6 + 2 (complement of 8) = 8

I do hope these examples have given you some amount of confidence and you are in a position to enjoy subtraction a little bit. By this time you must be finding it a little easier to work from left to right and cancelling tens in the answer rather than **borrowing** from the neighbouring number. Once you become fully used to it, you will find it far more natural and infinitely more foolproof than the older system. It has been estimated that 90 per cent of all mistakes in subtraction happen due to forgetting to borrow or borrowing too much. Since this method eliminates borrowing altogether, this method gives you accurate and faster result.

Handling Slashed Zero (∅)

There is absolutely no need to worry when you get a slashed zero in between the operation. Reduce the value to the left by 1 which in turn will make slashed zero 9.

$$2\cancel{0}4 = 1\cancel{2}_94 = 194$$

Example: 14567892 − 4567899 = ?

Solution:− 1 4 5 6 7 8 9 2
 −4 5 6 7 8 9 9
 $\overline{1\cancel{0}_9\cancel{0}_9\cancel{0}_9\cancel{0}_9\cancel{0}_9\cancel{0}_93}$
 = 9999993

Nothing from 1 = 1. Put down 1.

4 from 4 = 0. Put down 0

5 from 5 = 0. Put down 0 and so on, you get 0 until you come to the final column.

In the final column, 9 >2, hence 2 − 9 = 2 + 1(complement of 9) = 3. Put down 3. As discussed earlier, whenever you use complement for subtraction, cancel a 10 by slashing the digit on the left. The digit to the left is 0. Slash it. Whenever you slash a 0, you must go back and slash the digit to the left of it too. The next digit is also a 0, so you have to keep on slashing until you slash a digit that is not zero, and here you find the first digit from the left which is not a zero, so this too will be slashed by making 1 into 0 and all other 0s into 9.

Example:− 4573289 − 258684 = ?

Solution:- 4 5 7 3 2 8 9
 − 2 5 8 6 8 4
 4 3 2̸₁5̸₄ 6 0 5

Here,

4 − nothing = 4

5 − 2 = 3

7 − 5 = 2̸ = 1 (complement is used in next operation so this digit is 1 after slashing)

3 − 8 = 3 + 2 (Complement of 8) = 5̸ = 4 (complement in next operation)

2 − 6 = 2 + 4 (Complement of 6) = 6

8 − 8 = 0

9 − 4 = 5

Before I ask you about your opinion about the method discussed let me put few examples for you to practise and get a command over the method.

a) 12345   b) 86406   c) 9000045   d) 88888888
   −4567   −37606   −7865745   −24569997

So, what is your view on the above method of subtraction? Isn't it cool?

This is flawless and quicker than the traditional method and with a little practice you can do most of the operations in your mind without using pen and pad and can proudly say SUBTRACTION IS FUN.

3

Multiplication Is Easy

Multiplication is one of the main pillars of the four fundamental mathematical operations (Add, Subtract, Multiply and Divide). Multiplication in simple words is nothing but repeated addition. When we say 5 times 5 is 25 we are either multiplying 5 by 5 or adding 5 times 5. In both the conditions the result will be same.

$5 + 5 + 5 + 5 + 5 = 5 \times 5 = 25$

Let's look at the other side of the coin. Suppose you are given this particular problem to solve:–

$545 + 545 + 876 + 124 + 876 + 876 + 545 + 545 + 876 + 124 + 545 + 124 = ?$

If you observe the question minutely, you will find the repetition of only three numbers (545, 876 and 124) here. If you understand multiplication you will not add them, on the contrary you will count the number of times a particular number is repeated and multiply them before adding. Here 545 is repeated 5 times, 876 is repeated 4 times and 124 is repeated 3 times.

Hence,

$545 + 545 + 876 + 124 + 876 + 876 + 545 + 545 + 876 + 124 + 545 + 124 = 545 \times 5 + 876 \times 4 + 124 \times 3$
$= 2725 + 3504 + 372 = 6601$

This shows that multiplication comes very handy in handling the calculation.

Why Is Multiplication Important in our Daily Life

- Our brain is like a computer. Whatever you put into it, will most probably remain there for a long period of time. The multiplication table which you learned in KG will remain in your mind for long and whenever you need to sum up a result like calculating the cost of pizzas and burgers while eating out at a cafeteria you will need the help of multiplication.
- Multiplication helps you to understand your grocery bills, electricity bills and most importantly your mobile bills, when you recharge your mobile with call cutter top-up to reduce your call bills.
- In stock market, multiplication is like breathing. The mantra for getting successful in business is to consolidate your multiplication techniques.

Areas where Multiplication Is Essential:–

- In solving word problems
- Fractions—converting from mixed fractions to improper fractions
- Finding the areas and volumes of a figure
- In long division
- Calculating the interest rate: either simple or compound
- Combination and permutations and in many more such areas

Now the big question is—if multiplication is the backbone of doing calculations, why should we not learn some techniques that can help us to multiply super fast and that too without mistakes?

Components of Multiplication

```
      4 2 3 5  ──────▶  Multiplicand
    X   2 5   ──────▶  Multiplier
    2 1 1 7 5
  + 8 4 7 0 X
  1 0 5 8 7 5  ──────▶  Product
```

I still remember one of my Vedic maths lectures when I was asked a very simple question by a class 6 student, which I am putting here for you.

Sir, why Do We Put Cross Marks in Multiplication After Every Operation We Perform?

I think many of us do not know the answer of this simple question. At first glance, this question can be termed as silly but until you get the answer of most of such silly questions you will not be able to love mathematics. The simple answer is—once we do the multiplication of unit digit, we put a cross mark under unit digit to avoid any confusion while multiplying the ten's digit of multiplier with multiplicand. After the multiplication of ten's digit is over, we put a cross mark below the ten's digit and move to find the product of next digit at hundred place.

```
        3 4 5
      X 2 5 6
        2 0 7 0
      1 7 2 5 X
    + 6 9 0 X X
      8 8 3 2 0
```

Understand the basic structure of 256. In place value system 256 can be explicitly written as

$$256 = 2 \times 100 + 5 \times 10 + 6$$

Now look at the above multiplication and you will find that 5 of 256 is at the ten's place. Hence a cross is marked below the unit place and the final product of 345 × 5 begins from the ten's place. Similarly, 2 of 256 is at the hundred place and so is its product written from the hundred place and hence two cross marks one below the unit pace and another below the ten's place are made.

Do you know that primitive people used to count with the help of fingers and until the introduction of Hindu-Arabic numeral system in the Western world they used to do simple arithmetical calculation using fingers? Even today, most of the people do multiplication of two digits using their fingers. Have you seen a street hawker calculating the price of fruits, vegetables using a calculator? Probably not, because they can do the same multiplication using fingers faster than a calculator.

Multiplication Using Fingers

Case 1:– Multiplication of a single digit number by nine
Multiplication using fingers just requires the knowledge of table up to 4 × 4 and multiplication of any number by 10.
Let's start the multiplication using hands.

- Mark your fingers with numbers 1 to 10

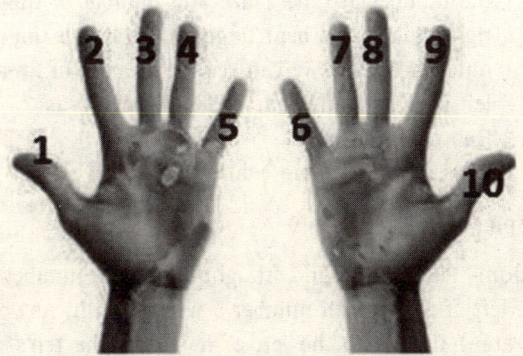

Figure 3.1

Multiplication Is Easy 23

- Bend the finger of your left hand with the appropriate number which you are going to multiply with 9. Suppose we have to multiply 3 by 9; we will then bend the left finger with 3 marked on it as shown in the image below.

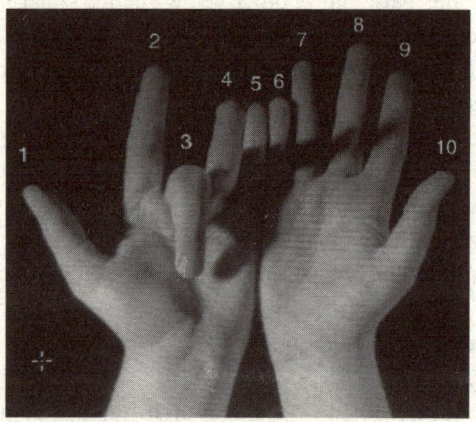

Figure 3.2: *3 × 9*

- Count the number of fingers on either side of the bent finger. Number of fingers on the left part will tell you the number at ten's place and number of fingers at the right side of the bent finger will tell you the number at unit place. Here we can see the number of fingers on the left side is 2 and that of the right side is 7.
  Hence, 3 × 9 = 27
  Let's take one more example.

Example:– Multiply 5 by 9

Solution:– Place your hand straight. Count the number of fingers to the left of finger with number 5 written on it. As you can see there are 4 fingers to the left of it. Hence the ten's digit is 4. Now count the number of fingers to the right side of that finger.

Here you can see 5 fingers to the right side giving you the unit place of the product. Hence, 5 × 9 = 45.

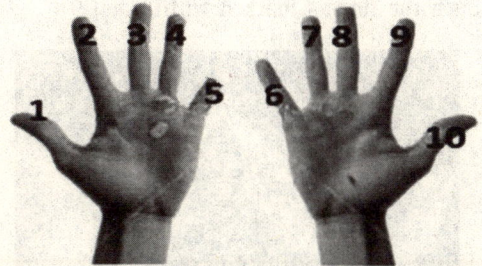

Figure 3.3

Case 2:– Multiplying two numbers from 6 × 6 to 10 × 10
Rule:– Suppose you have to multiply two numbers x and y where 6≤ x ≤ 10 and 6 ≤ y ≤ 10 then the rule will be as follows:

- Mark the fingers with numbers 6 to 10 on both the hands.

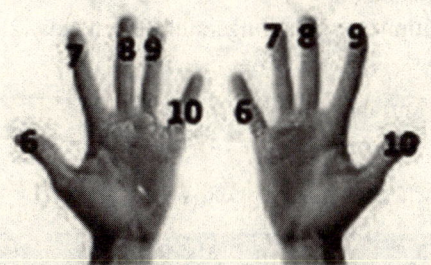

Figure 3.4

- Touch the corresponding finger and bend the fingers below the touched fingers.
- Count the number of unbent fingers. This will tell you the digit to be put at ten's place.
- Multiply the bent fingers of both the hands to obtain the digit at the one's place.

Multiplication Is Easy 25

Example:- Multiply 8 by 9

Solution:-
- Touch the fingers marked with 8 and 9

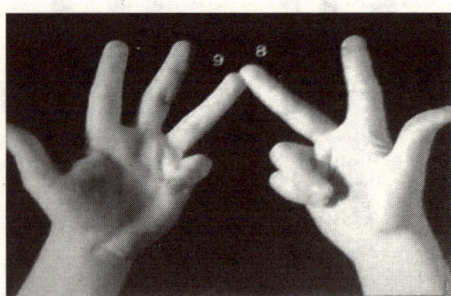

Figure 3.5

- Bend the fingers below it.
- Count the unbent fingers in both hands and get the digit at the ten's place. Here the sum of unbent fingers in both the hands is $4 + 3 = 7$
- Multiply the bent fingers of both hands. $2 \times 1 = 2$
  Hence, $8 \times 9 = 72$

Example:- Multiply 8 by 8

Solution:-
- Touch the finger marked with 8

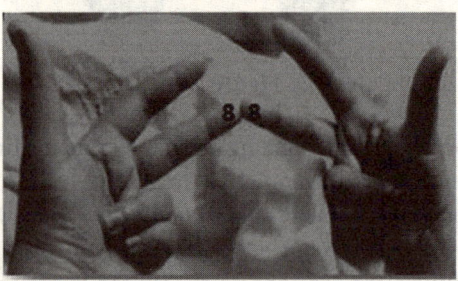

Figure 3.6

- Bend the fingers below the touched fingers.
- Count the unbent fingers in both hands and get the digit at the ten's place. Here the sum of unbent fingers in both the hands is 3 + 3 = 6.
- Multiply the bent fingers of both hands; 2 × 2 = 4. Hence, 8 × 8 = 64.

Case 3:– Multiplying two numbers from 11 × 11 to 15 × 15

Rule:– Suppose you have to multiply two numbers x and y where 11≤ x ≤ 15 and 11 ≤ y ≤ 15 then the rule will be as follows:

- Mark the finger with numbers 11 to 15 in both the hands.
- Touch the corresponding finger and bend fingers below the touched fingers.
- Count the number of unbent fingers. Multiply it by 10.
- Multiply the unbent fingers of both hands.
- Add 100 to the previous two steps to get the final answer.

Example:– Multiply 13 by 12

Solution:–

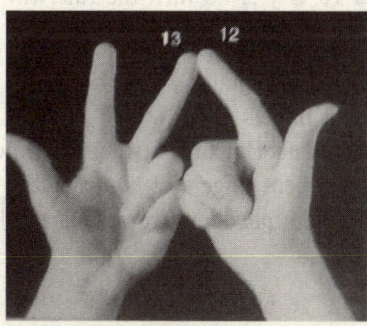

Figure 3.7

- Number of unbent fingers in both the hands are 3 and 2 respectively. As the rule says; we multiply the number of unbent fingers by 10.

$$5 \times 10 = 50$$

Multiplication Is Easy 27

- Multiply the number of unbent fingers.

$$3 \times 2 = 6$$

- Add 100 to the previous two results to get the final result
  Hence, $13 \times 12 = 100 + 50 + 6 = 156$

Example:– Multiply 15 by 13

Solution:– Touch the finger marking 15 and 13 of both hands.
- Number of unbent fingers = 8
- Multiply the number of unbent fingers = $5 \times 3 = 15$

Since the product of unbent fingers is kept at the unit place so 15 will make the number 8 at ten's place richer by 1 making the ten's place 9

- Add 100 to the previous two results
  = $100 + 80 + 15 = 195$

Case 4:– Multiplying two numbers from 16×16 to 20×20

Rule:– Suppose you have to multiply two numbers x and y where $16 \leq x \leq 20$ and $16 \leq y \leq 20$ then the rule will be as follows:

- Mark the finger with numbers 16 to 20 in both the hands.
- Touch the corresponding finger and bend fingers below the touched fingers.
- Count the number of unbent fingers. Multiply it by 20.
- Multiply the bent fingers of both hands.
- Add 200 to the previous two results to obtain the final answer.

Example:– Multiply 16 by 19

Solution:– In the given picture below, we see

- Number of unbent fingers = 5
- Number of bent fingers in each hands are 4 and 1 respectively.
- Multiply the number of unbent fingers with 20.

$$5 \times 20 = 100$$

- Product of bent fingers on both hands = 4 × 1 = 4
- Add 200

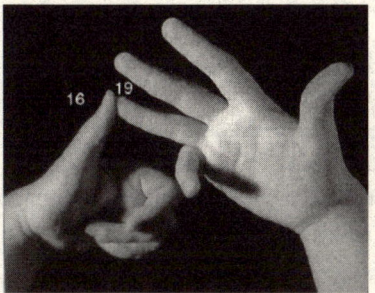

Figure 3.8

- Hence the result of 16 × 19 = 200 + 100 + 4 = 304

Here are some problems to try by yourself. Instead of taking the help of a calculator you can use the finger method of multiplication. Write the answer on a piece of paper so that you can check your answer.

a) 8 × 9 =   b) 7 × 9 =   c) 7 × 7 =
d) 5 × 9 =   e) 8 × 7 =   f) 11 × 12 =
g) 12 × 14 =   h) 15 × 14 =   i) 16 × 16 =
j) 17 × 16 =   k) 19 × 18 =   l) 17 × 18 =

Now let's move to the normal way of multiplication as we are taught in our school curriculum but in a super-fast way which will help you to multiply two numbers in seconds. I do hope that once you adopt this system of multiplication you will soon be able to do all steps mentally in no time.

Do you remember the multiplication table up to 9?

If your answer is YES, then I promise you that these techniques will help you to multiply any numbers in seconds. Simply follow the instructions and practise the sum for better understanding. In order to understand multiplication better and better we will learn the technique in segments.

Multiplication Is Easy

Multiplication of Numbers up to 10

Example:– 8 × 6 = ?

Solution:– As you can see both the numbers are below 10. Let's take the first number 8. How many more do you need to make 10? The answer is 2. Write 2 below the circle 8. Now go to the other number 6. How many more do you need to make 10? The answer is 4. Write it below in the circle the number 6. The whole operation will now look like...

$$8 \times 6$$
$$②\quad ④$$

Now subtract the numbers diagonally.
8 – 4 = 4   or   6 – 2 = 4
Now multiply the two circled numbers.
2 × 4 = 8
Hence, 8 × 6 = 48
Let's take another example.

Example:– Multiply 7 by 9

Solution:– Write the difference of the number from 10 in the circle below. 7 is 3 less than 10 and 9 is 1 less than 10.

$$7 \times 9$$
$$③\quad ①$$

Subtract the number diagonally.

7 – 1 = 6 or 9 – 3 = 6

Now multiply the two circled numbers.

3 × 1 = 3

Hence,

9 × 7 = 63

Now let's look at the problem in another way. What we have done in the previous two examples is to take difference from 10.

Take it the other way. Let's consider 10 as the base and now we shall find the differences of the numbers to be multiplied by the reference base. We are now extending the multiplication of numbers to the reference base 10, 100, 1000...

Rule:–

- Take the difference of the number from the designated base which is the multiple of 10 or 10^n, where n is any natural number.
- Do diagonal operation.
- Multiply the result obtained in the previous step by the reference base.
- Take the multiplication of the differences which may be written either with plus (+) or minus (−) sign.
- Add the two results to get the answer.

Example:– Multiply 12 by 13

Solution:– Here the two numbers 12 and 13 are more than the base 10

$12 - 10 = + 2$
$13 - 10 = + 3$

Place the differences of the number adjacent to the numbers to be multiplied.

12 +2
13 +3

The diagonal operation yields the result–

$12 + 3 = 15$ or $13 + 2 = 15$

Multiply the result by reference base 10

$15 \times 10 = 150$

Take the multiplication of differences.

$2 \times 3 = 6$

Add the two results.

$150 + 6 = 156$

Hence, $12 \times 13 = 156$

Example:– Multiply 14 by 17

Solution:– Here the two numbers 14 and 17 are more than the base 10

$14 - 10 = + 4$
$17 - 10 = + 7$

Place the differences of the numbers adjacent to the numbers to be multiplied.

$14 + 4$
$\underline{17 + 7}$

The diagonal operation yields the following result
$14 + 7 = 21$ or $17 + 4 = 21$
Multiply the result by reference base 10
$21 \times 10 = 210$
Take the multiplication of differences.
$4 \times 7 = 28$
Add the two results.
$210 + 28 = 238$
Hence, $14 \times 17 = 238$

Example:– Multiply 92 by 98

Solution:– Here the two numbers 92 and 98 are less than the base 100

$92 - 100 = -8$
$98 - 100 = -2$

Place the differences of the numbers adjacent to the numbers to be multiplied.

$92 \; -8$
$\underline{98 \; -2}$

The diagonal operation yields the following result
$92 - 2 = 90$ or $98 - 8 = 90$
Multiply the result by reference base 100
$90 \times 100 = 9000$

Take the multiplication of differences.
$-8 \times -2 = 16$
Add the two results.
$9000 + 16 = 9016$
Hence, $92 \times 98 = 9016$

Example:– Multiply 96 by 95

Solution:– Here the two numbers 96 and 95 are less than the base 100

$96 - 100 = -4$
$95 - 100 = -5$

Place the differences of the number adjacent to the numbers to be multiplied.

96 −4
95 −5

The diagonal operation yields the following result
$96 - 5 = 91$ or $95 - 4 = 91$
Multiply the result by reference base 100
$91 \times 100 = 9100$
Take the multiplication of differences.
$-4 \times -5 = 20$
Add the two results.
$9100 + 20 = 9120$
Hence, $96 \times 95 = 9120$

Example:– Multiply 962 by 998

Solution:– Here the two numbers 962 and 998 are less than the base 1000

$962 - 1000 = -38$
$998 - 1000 = -2$

Place the differences of the number adjacent to the numbers to be multiplied.

962 −38
998 −2

The diagonal operation yields the result
962 − 2 = 960 or 998 − 38 = 960
Multiply the result by reference base 100
960 × 1000 = 960000
Take the multiplication of differences.
−38 × −2 = 76
Add the two results.
960000 + 76 = 960076
Hence, 962 × 998 = 96076

Example:− Multiply 108 by 97

Solution:− Here the first number 108 is more than the reference base whereas 97 is less than the reference base 100.

108 − 100 = +8
97 − 100 = −3

Place the differences of the number adjacent to the numbers to be multiplied.

108 +8
<u>97 −3</u>

The diagonal operation yields the following result
108 − 3 = 105 or 97 + 8 = 105
Multiply the result by reference base 100
105 × 100 = 10500
Take the multiplication of differences.
+ 8 × −3 = −24
Add the two results.
10500 −24 = 10476
Hence, 108 × 97 = 10476

Example:− Multiply 1022 by 993

Solution:− Here the first number 1022 is more than the reference base 1000 whereas 993 is less than the reference base 1000.

1022 − 1000 = +22
993 − 1000 = −7

Place the differences of the number adjacent to the numbers to be multiplied.

1022 +22
993 −7

The diagonal operation yields the following result

1022 − 7 = 1015   or   993 + 22 = 1015

Multiply the result by reference base 1000

1015 × 1000 = 1015000

Take the multiplication of differences.

+ 22 × −7 = −154

Add the two results.

1015000 −154 = 1014846

Hence, 1022 × 993 = 1014846

Can You Do These Operations in your Head?

Certainly!

Solving problems in your head plays an important role. I would request you to go through the above examples once more. For your convenience, I am putting another example for your better understanding.

Example:– Multiply 97 by 92

Your visualization is very important in calculating faster. You can see that both the numbers are nearer to the base 100 and both the numbers are lesser than the base. Take the difference of either of the number from the reference base and add to the other number. The difference of 92 from the base 100 is −8 and the difference of 97 from the base is −3. Add −8 to 97; i.e. 97 − 8 = 89. These operations can be done mentally in no time. Now multiply the result with the reference base 100 to get the answer 8900. Finally add the product of differences; i.e. − 8 × − 3 = 24

Hence, your answer is 97 × 92 = 8924

Let's practise some problems before we move on to the next method.

a) 14 × 15 b) 17 × 19 c) 96 × 94
d) 106 × 108 e) 94 × 108 f) 98 × 99
g) 995 × 987 h) 982 × 1007 i) 1004 × 1042

Now let's move a step ahead and see whether the above problems can be done more quickly.

Example:– Multiply 94 by 93

Solution:– As done before we shall write the difference of the number multiplied with its base in the first step.

Number	Difference from Reference base (100)	Difference of difference from nearest base 10
94	−6	−4
93	−7	−3

The second difference of difference lets you multiply easily if you don't remember the table of 6 or 7. Take the diagonal difference as done before and write the result.

94 − 7 = 87 or 93 − 6 = 87

Multiply the result with the first reference base 100, i.e. 87 × 100 = 8700

In order to simplify the multiplication of 6 × 7 we take the second difference and do the same operations.

Diagonal difference	Multiplication by base 10	Product of differences	Sum
6 − 3 = 3	3 × 10 = 30	4 × 3 = 12	30 + 12

Hence, 94 × 93 = 8700 + 42 = 8742

The method used above shows the multiplication of numbers which are nearer to the base 10 or 100. But what about multiplying numbers that are around 20, 30, 40 or 50? Can we still use this method?

Yes, certainly we can.

Have you ever thought why did we choose the reference base as 10, 100 or 1000 in the above examples?

The purpose was very clear. We chose reference number in the power of 10 because it is easy to multiply by those numbers. This method will work just as well with other reference numbers, but we must choose numbers that are easy to multiply by. In order to multiply a number by 20, we will first multiply the number by 2 and then by 10.

Example:– Multiply 24 by 26

Solution:– Since both the numbers are very close to 20, we will take the reference base as 20. As discussed before, we will take the difference of the numbers to be multiplied by with the reference base and write them adjacent to the numbers. 24 is 4 more than 20 and 26 is 6 more than 20.

24 +4
26 +6

Do the diagonal operation as done before:

24 + 6 = 30   or   26 + 4 = 30

Multiply the answer by reference base 20. To do this, we first multiply it by 2 and then by 10.

30 × 2 = 60   and   60 ×10 = 600

Multiply the difference and add as we did in the previous so many examples.

4 × 6 = 24   and   600 + 24 = 624

Hence, 24 × 26 = 624

Example:– Multiply 21 by 36

Solution:– Take 20 as the reference base and write the difference of the numbers to be multiplied by 20.

21 +1
36 +16

Add diagonally, then multiply the result by the reference number.

21 + 16 = 37   or   36 + 1 = 37
37 × 20 = 740

Multiply the difference written adjacent to the numbers and add to the previous result.

1 × 16 = 16
740 + 16 = 756
Hence, 21 × 36 = 756

Taking 20 as reference number will take care of numbers up to 30, but if the numbers are higher then you can take 50 as a reference number, as it is easy to multiply a number by 50 because 50 = ½ of 100.

Taking 50 as Reference Base

Example:– Multiply 46 by 48

Solution:– Both the numbers to be multiplied are close to the base 50. Take the difference of the numbers from the reference base and write it adjacent to the numbers.

46 −4
48 −2

Subtract diagonally as there is a negative sign in the differences.

46 − 2 = 44   or   48 − 4 = 44
Multiply 44 by 100 and divide the result obtained by 2.
44 × 100 = 4400
4400 ÷ 2 = 2200
Multiply the differences.
−4 × − 2 = 8
Add 8 to the previous result 2200
2200 + 8 = 2208
Hence, 46 × 48 = 2208

Example:– Multiply 56 by 59

Solution:– Take the difference of the numbers from the reference base 50 and write it adjacent to the numbers.

56 +6
59 +9

Add diagonally as there is a positive sign in the differences.

56 + 9 = 65   or   59 + 6 = 65

Multiply 65 by 100 and divide the result obtained by 2.

65 × 100 = 4400

6500 ÷ 2 = 3250

Multiply the differences.

6 × 9 = 54

Add 54 to the previous result 3250

3250 + 54 = 3304

Hence, 56 × 59 = 3304

Let's try two more questions.

Example:– Multiply 58 by 69

Solution:– Take the difference of the numbers from the reference base 50 and write it adjacent to the numbers.

58 +8
69 +19

Add diagonally as there is a positive sign in the differences.

58 +19 = 77   or   69 + 8 = 77

Multiply 77 by 100 and divide the result obtained by 2.

77 × 100 = 7700

7700 ÷ 2 = 3850

Multiply the differences.

8 × 19 = 152

Add 152 to the previous result 3850

3850 + 152 = 4002

Hence, 56 × 59 = 3304

Example:– Multiply 47 by 63

Solution:– Take the difference of the numbers from the reference base 50 and write it adjacent to the numbers.

Multiplication Is Easy 39

47 −3
63 +13
Add / subtract diagonally.
47 + 13 = 60 or 63 − 3 = 60
Multiply 60 by 100 and divide the result obtained by 2.
60 × 100 = 6000
6000 ÷ 2 = 3000
Multiply the differences.
−3 × 13 = −39
Subtract 39 from the previous result 3000
3000 − 39 = 2961
Hence, 47 × 63 = 2961

Now it is time to practise. So be ready to do the calculation in your head.

a) 46 × 47   b) 51 × 55   c) 47 × 49
d) 44 × 44   e) 51 × 68   f) 54 × 72

I think you have understood the simple multiplication technique and are in a position to extend the base and feel comfortable in multiplying two numbers which are close to the base 200 or 500 in the same fashion. Let me take some examples and make the calculation easier for you.

Example:– Multiply 518 by 516

Solution:– Take the difference of the numbers from the reference base 500 and write it adjacent to the numbers.
518 +18
516 +16
Add diagonally as there is a positive sign in the differences.
518 + 16 = 534 or 516 + 18 = 534
Multiply 534 by 1000 and divide the result obtained by 2.
534 × 1000 = 534000
534000 ÷ 2 = 267000
Multiply the differences.

18 × 16 = ?

Do the multiplication of 18 and 16 as done at the beginning of this chapter.

18 +8
16 +6

This time the base is taken as 10.

Add diagonally 18 + 6 = 24.
Multiply the result by 10 = 24× 10 = 240
Multiply the differences; 8 × 6 = 48
Add 240 and 48 = 240 + 48 = 288

In order to get the final result add 267000 and 288—267000 + 288 = 267288

Hence, 516 × 518 = 267288

Multiplication Using Two Reference Bases

In the above discussion we have seen that multiplying with reference number is a child's play so long as the numbers to be multiplied are closer to the reference base. Now let's consider a case when the numbers to be multiplied stand nowhere near the base.

Example:– Multiply 17 by 89

The big question here is

a) Which reference number would we choose?
b) Is it possible to multiply two numbers that are not close to each other by the simple method and yet be able to find the answer in seconds?

Don't worry. We can take two different reference numbers and do the operation quite easily. Let me put the rule for you which will help you to understand the examples better.

Suppose you have to multiply 23 by 67. Here the two reference numbers will be 20 and 60 because 23 is closer to base 20 and 67 is closer to base 60. From the two reference numbers, we choose the easiest one to take as the principal base. The second reference number should be the multiple of the first. Here the second reference base $60 = 3 \times 20$.

Example:– Multiply 7 by 29

Solution:– The first number 7 is closer to base 10 and the second number 29 is close to base 30 (which is 3×10). We write the second reference number in its broken form in the parenthesis.

Reference base	Smallest number	Second number
$3 \times 10 = 30$	7	29
Difference from base	–3	–1
Difference × Multiplicative factor of 2nd reference number	$3 \times 3 = 9$	
Diagonal difference	$29 - 9 = 20$	
× 1st base reference number	$20 \times 10 = 200$	
Product of differences of the bases	$-3 \times -1 = 3$	
Add the last two results	$200 + 3 = 203$	

Let's understand the modus operandi shown in the above table.

- Take the differences of both the numbers to be multiplied from their nearest bases. If the number to be multiplied is more than the base then use + sign otherwise a minus sign will be used.
- The difference of the smaller number will be multiplied by the multiplicative factor of second reference base.
- Do the diagonal operation (plus / minus) of second number with the result obtained in 2nd step and multiply the result with the smaller base.
- Add the product of differences of the bases to the previous result.

Let's take an example for a better understanding of the concept. Though initially you may feel uncomfortable in dealing with the situation, very soon you will adapt to the technique and enjoy doing multiplication with this method.

Example:– Multiply 16 by 54

Solution:–

Reference base	Smallest number	Second number
5 × 10 = 50	16	54
Difference from base	+6	+4
Difference × Multiplicative factor of 2nd reference number	6 × 5 = 30	
Diagonal operation	54 + 30 = 84	
× 1st base reference number	84 × 10 = 840	
Product of differences of the bases	6 × 4 = 24	
Add the last two results	840 + 24 = 864	

Example:– Multiply 32 by 89

Solution:– Here we have to take two different bases as the first number 32 is nearer to base 30 and the second number 89 is closer to base 90.

Reference base	Smallest number	Second number
3 × 30 = 90	32	89
Difference from base	+2	−1
Difference × Multiplicative factor of 2nd reference number	2 × 3 = 6	
Diagonal operation	89 + 6 = 95	

× 1st base reference number	$95 \times 30 = 2850$
Product of differences of the bases	$2 \times -1 = -2$
Add the last two results	$2850 - 2 = 2848$

Example:– Multiply 112 by 343

Solution:– Here the first number 112 is closer to base 100 but what about the other number 343? If you take the base 400 then the second number will be 57 less than its base which will create a problem in solving the problem in an easy manner. But if you take the base 350 then the calculation will be easier for you. Moreover 350 is 3½ times 100. Let's see the whole operation in tabular form.

Reference base	Smallest number	Second number
3½ × 100 = 350	112	343
Difference from base	+12	−7
Difference × Multiplicative factor of 2nd reference number	$12 \times 3½ = 36 + 6 = 42$	
Diagonal operation	$343 + 42 = 385$	
× 1st base reference number	$385 \times 100 = 38500$	
Product of differences of the bases	$12 \times -7 = -84$	
Add the last two results	$38500 - 84 = 38416$	

I do hope you are enjoying this unconventional method of multiplication. In order to make this journey a memorable one I am giving a very interesting multiplication technique that will make multiplication much easier. The best part of this method is that you need not think about the base anymore.

MULTIPLICATION (PART–II)

Multiplication as discussed in the previous chapter might have given you some amount of relief. You must be wondering if there is some other method which would make you feel more comfortable in doing multiplication without any pre-condition as laid down in the first part. Multiplication can be even more fun if you practise it using the method discussed here.

Dot and Stick Method of Multiplication

I call this method a panacea. The best part of this method is its simplicity and hassle-free operation. You need not worry about base number and other such things at all. I shall focus on multiplication of 2 × 2 to 4 × 4 in this chapter and give you an idea of how to extend the operation further and you can easily go through the operation according to your needs. Let's begin the journey of Dot and Stick Method.

2 × 1 Multiplication

The 2 × 1 will be an easy task if you do multiply each digit separately and keep writing the digit one below the other as shown in the illustration. The best part of this method is that you don't need to remember the carry part. Let's see the illustration here to understand the fact vividly. The dot operation of 2 × 1 will be as shown below.

Example:– Multiply 38 by 4

Solution:– Place the number on dots.

Multiplication Is Easy

```
    3   8
    •   •
    × •4
    ───
    3 2    (4 times 8 = 32)
  + 1 2    (4 times 3 = 12)
  ─────
  1 5 2
```

Example: Multiply 62 by 8

Solution:– Place the number on dots.

```
    6   2
    •   •
    × •8
    ───
    1 6    (8 times 2 = 16)
  + 4 8    (8 times 6 = 48)
  ─────
    4 9 6
```

Example:– Multiply 72 by 5

Solution:– Place the number on dots.

```
    7   2
    •   •
    × •5
    ───
    1 0    (5 times 2 = 10)
  + 3 5    (5 times 7 = 35)
  ─────
    3 6 0
```

2 × 2 Multiplication

The dot method of 2 × 2 is as follows-

This can also be done by the dot method shown below. There is no difference in either representations; the only difference is the way you do the calculation. Some people find it safe to write the multiplicand above and multiplier below it (as shown in the above diagram) whereas some people find it convenient to do multiplication by writing the multiplicand and multiplier in the same line as shown below. I will take one example where I would do the same multiplication on both representations of dots so that you can understand the fact clearly.

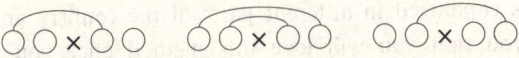

Rule:-

- First place the digits on the dots.
- Multiply the digits placed on arrow or arc and write the result below.
- Be careful in the second operation as here you have to do two operations simultaneously and add them.
- Place the result of each operation below the dots. When all operations have been finalized, add the results moving right to left, keeping only a single digit in each cell besides the left most.

Example:- Multiply 42 by 12

Solution:- I am doing this question by writing the multiplicand 42 above and multiplier 12 below it. First place the digits on the dots. It is not necessary in the long run as you can eventually do the whole operation in your mind without any mistake but for that you will have to practise at least 20 questions.

Hey, are you ready for the journey of fast calculation by riding the bullet train of multiplication?

Place the digits on the dots.

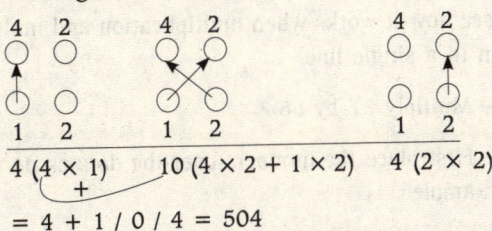

$= 4 + 1 / 0 / 4 = 504$

Though at first glance the method illustrated appears to be a lengthy process but believe me this will be one of the easiest processes once you go through the method minutely. I have noticed the change in accuracy and speed of students in my 180-odd seminars conducted in different parts of the country and I can assure you that you will love this method once you become habituated to do the calculation in your mind. You need not place these numbers on dots while doing the separate operations, on the contrary you will be able to do justice to the calculation in one go.

$$\begin{array}{r} 4 \quad 2 \\ \times \ 1 \ 2 \\ \hline 4/8 + 2/2 \\ = 4/10/2 \\ = 502 \end{array}$$

Let's see how it works when multiplication and multiplicand are written in a single line.

$$\underline{4\ 2 \times 1\ 2} \qquad \underline{4\ 2 \times 1\ 2} \qquad \underline{4\ 2 \times 1\ 2}$$
$$\quad 4 \qquad\qquad 8 + 2 = 10 \qquad\quad 4$$
$$= 5 \qquad\qquad\qquad 0 \qquad\qquad\qquad 4$$

I do hope that you have understood both the methods and enjoyed its operation. It is unique and simple in operation and fast in result. You just have to practise some questions to get mastery over this simple technique.

Let's take another example.

Let's see how it works when multiplication and multiplicand are written in a single line.

Example:– Multiply 87 by 56

Solution:– First place the numbers over the dots as done in the previous example

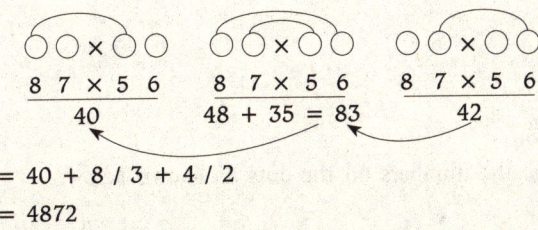

$= 40 + 8 / 3 + 4 / 2$

$= 4872$

Example:– Multiply 93 by 67

Solution:– First place the numbers over the dots as done in the previous example

$= 54 + 8 / 1 + 2 / 1$

$= 6231$

To conceptualize the method let's practise some 2 by 2 multiplication.

a) 76 × 53   b) 84 × 77   c) 79 × 68
d) 57 × 34   e) 38 × 58   f) 56 × 86

3 × 3 Multiplication Method

The 3 × 3 multiplication is nothing but the extension of the previous operation as the modus operandi of both the methods are alike. In order to understand the concept I shall first explain the example in detail, and I am that hopeful you will enjoy it better than the traditional method taught in your classroom.

Multiplication of 3-digit number

Example:– Multiply 213 by 114

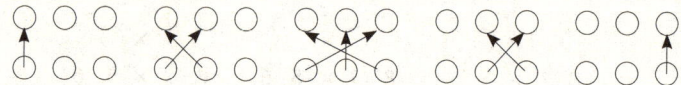

Solution:-

Arrange the numbers on the dots as shown below.

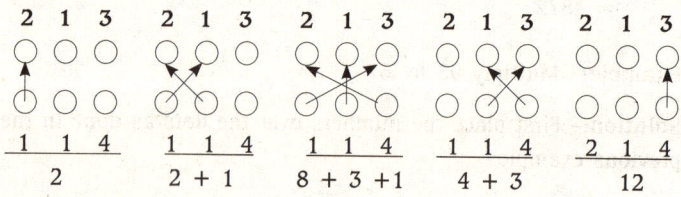

Arrange each product with vertical separators as shown below.
= 2 / 3 / 12 / 7 / 12
= 2 4 2 8 2

Example:- Multiply 786 by 458

Solution:-

Arrange the numbers on the dots as shown below.

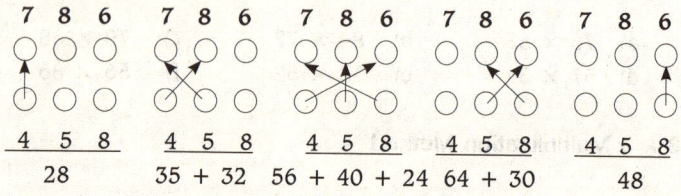

Arrange each product with vertical separators as shown below.
= 28 / 67 / 120 / 94 / 48

= 359988

If you don't wish to add the product as shown above then there is another way to find the answer but here you will have to be careful in placing the digits. Let's see how to put the numbers and place them one below the other before finally summing up the digits.

```
  2 8
  3 5 ⎫
  3 2 ⎭
    5 6 ⎫
    4 0 ⎬
    2 4 ⎭
      3 0 ⎫
      6 4 ⎭
+       4 8
3 5 9 9 8 8
```

Example:– Multiply 956 by 754

Solution:–

Arrange the numbers on the dots as shown below.

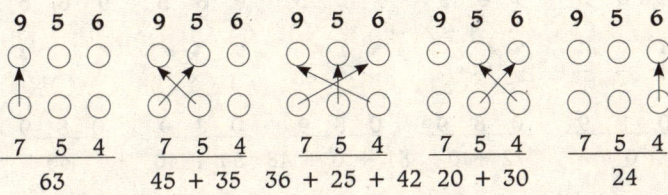

Arrange each product with vertical separators as shown below.

= 63 / 80 /103 / 50 / 24

= 720824

The whole operation can be done in a single line.

Example:– Multiply 247 by 989.

Solution:– The whole operation of dot and cross method is done here in one line.

```
        2 4 7
      × 9 8 9
 ₁8 | ₅2 | ₁₁3 | ₉2 | ₆3
        8  2  3  2  3
   +    1  5 11  9  6
        2  4  4  2  8  3
```

Multiplication Is Easy

Illustration:– Here the unit digit is written at the top and the left out digits of each column are written below. For the convenience of readers, unit digits are written in bold and other digits are written in subscript. Moreover, as discussed above the single digit in each column should be written and the other digits should be transferred to the left column and added. Here I have written the digits to be transferred in the second column.

Example:– Multiply 965 by 89

Solution:– This is a 3 × 2 digits multiplication so put a zero in front of 43, making it 043 and now apply the above 3 × 3 operation technique. Arrange the numbers on the dots as shown below.

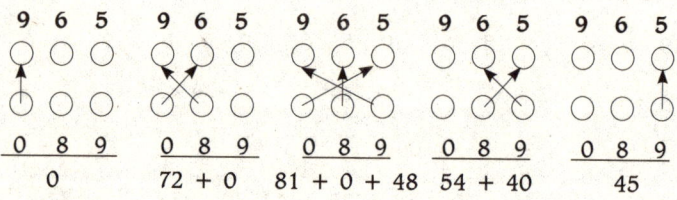

= 0 | 72 | 129 | 94 | 45
= 85885

Let's do some practice problems for better clarity of the modus operandi.

a) 653 × 777 b) 876 × 964 c) 987 × 654
d) 852 × 707 e) 549 × 816 f) 893 × 629

After learning these simple ways of 2 × 2 and 3 × 3 multiplications, I am extending it to 4 × 4 operation. The 4 × 4 operation is shown here on dot and stick for your better understanding.

Multiplication of 4-digit numbers

Example: Multiply 5734 by 5845

Solution:– Arranging the numbers on the dots.

5 7 3 4	5 7 3 4	5 7 3 4	5 7 3 4	5 7 3 4	5 7 3 4	5 7 3 4
5 8 4 5	5 8 4 5	5 8 4 5	5 8 4 5	5 8 4 5	5 8 4 5	5 8 4 5
25	40+35	20+15+56	25+20+28+24	35+32+12	15+16	20

Arrange the numbers in vertical separators.

25 / 75 / 91 / 97 / 79 / 31 / 20

= 33515230

Example: Multiply 7089 by 4512

Solution:– Arranging the numbers on the dots.

7 0 8 9	7 0 8 9	7 0 8 9	7 0 8 9	7 0 8 9	7 0 8 9	7 0 8 9
4 5 1 2	4 5 1 2	4 5 1 2	4 5 1 2	4 5 1 2	4 5 1 2	4 5 1 2
28	35+0	7+32+0	14+36+0+40	0+45+8	16+9	18

Arrange the numbers in vertical separators.

28 / 35 / 39 / 90 / 53 / 25 / 18

= 31985568

I do hope that the method discussed above will make your journey of multiplication a little bit more comfortable and you will enjoy doing your calculation through it with super speed and accuracy. In the latter part of this book I shall focus on a special chapter which will help to ensure whether the calculations you have done is right or wrong. Before I wind up this chapter let's do some practice problems.

a) 7856 × 6542 b) 8887 × 5641 c) 9087 × 8654
d) 6556 × 7609 e) 8609 × 9121 f) 6575 × 8633

4

Multiplication Without Paper

Multiplication can be made an interesting exercise by learning some tricks. In the last two chapters we have seen that there are several methods, which reduce the calculation time by one tenth. Don't you think that you should have knowledge of some super-duper trick which can save your time and using which multiplication can be done mentally without using pen and paper?

There are hundreds of such magical tricks which help one calculate mentally and without pen and paper. Do you know what is more interesting here is that there is absolutely no chance of making a mistake? Let me ask you a simple question first:-

What is 100 times 456789?

I am really not joking guys, despite the fact that I know you can do this multiplication in the fraction of a second by just putting two zeros after 456789—4567890. The fact of the matter is that when you are asked to multiply a number by the multiple of 10, like 10, 100, 1000, 10000... you just put the required number of zeros behind the number to be multiplied by noticing how many numbers of zeros are in there in the multiplier which is a multiple of 10. Likewise, the method discussed here will let you get the answer in seconds.

Hey guys, are you ready for the journey of fun multiplication? If your answer is a big YES, then here I begin.

1. When the sum of unit digits is 10 and ten's digits are same

Rule:- a) The answer will have two parts. Multiply the unit parts. The product should have exactly two digits. If you get a lesser digit put a zero before.

b) Second Part = Ten's digit × (Ten's digit + 1)

Example:- 42 × 48 = ?

Solution:- Here the sum of unit digits is 10 (2 + 8 = 10) and ten's digit in both multiplicand and multiplier are same.
　　Unit Part = 2 × 8 = 16
　　Second Part = 4 × 5 = 20
　　Hence, 42 × 48 = 2016

Example:- 74 × 76 = ?

Solution:- Sum of unit digit = 10 (4 + 6 = 10) and ten's digit in both multiplicand and multiplier are same (7).
　　Unit Part = 4 × 6 = 24
　　Second Part = 7 × 8 = 56
　　Hence, 74 × 76 = 5624

Example:- 99 × 91 = ?

Solution:- Sum of unit digits = 10 (9 + 1 = 10) and ten's digit in both multiplicand and multiplier are same (9).
　　Unit Part = 9 × 1 = 09 (In order to fulfil the condition of two digits in the product 0 is put before 9)
　　Second Part = 9 × 10 = 90
　　Hence, 99 × 91 = 9009

2. Sum of ten's digits is 10 and unit digits are same

Rule:- The answer will have two parts
　　a) Left Hand Side (LHS) = Product of ten's digits + unit digit

Right Hand Side (RHS) = Product of unit digits
Always remember there should be exactly two digits in the RHS. In case there is a single digit in RHS, put a zero before the product you get

Example:– $84 \times 24 = ?$

Solution:– Sum of ten's digits = 10 (8+2 = 10) and unit digit in multiplicand and multiplier is same (4)
LHS = Product of ten's digits + unit digit = $8 \times 2 + 4 = 20$
RHS = Product of unit digits = $4 \times 4 = 16$
Hence, $84 \times 24 = 2016$

Example:– $93 \times 13 = ?$

Solution:– Sum of ten's digits = 10 (9+1 = 10) and unit digit in multiplicand and multiplier is same (3)
LHS = Product of ten's digits + unit digit = $9 \times 1 + 3 = 12$
RHS = Product of unit digits = $3 \times 3 = 09$
(one zero is put due to less number of digits in the product)
Hence, $93 \times 13 = 1209$

Example:– $75 \times 35 = ?$

Solution:– Sum of ten's digits = 10 (7 + 3 = 10) and unit digit in multiplicand and multiplier is same (5)
LHS = Product of ten's digits + unit digit = $7 \times 3 + 5 = 26$
RHS = Product of unit digits = $5 \times 5 = 25$
Hence, $75 \times 35 = 2625$

3. When the difference between the digits to be multiplied is 1

When two consecutive numbers are to be multiplied, follow this technique for quicker multiplication.
   a) Square the smaller/ greater number.
   b) Add / subtract the smaller/ larger number to the previous result

Example:– Multiply 23 by 24

Solution:– a) Square the smaller number = 23 × 23 = 529
b) Add the smaller number to the previous result
= 529 + 23 = 552
Hence, 23 × 24 = 552

Example:– Multiply 75 by 76

Solution:– a) Square the smaller number = 75 × 75 = 5625
b) Add the smaller number to the previous result
= 5625 + 75 = 5700
Hence, 75 × 76 = 5700

Example:– Multiply 95 by 94

Solution:– a) Square the larger number = 95 × 95 = 9025
b) Subtract the larger number from the previous result = 9025 − 95 = 8930
Hence, 95 × 94 = 8930

4. When the difference between the digits to be multiplied is 2

a) Find the mean and square it. The mean of two numbers a and b = a + b / 2
b) Subtract 1

Example:– Multiply 25 by 27

Solution:– a) Mean = 25 + 27 / 2 = 26. (Mean can be found by adding 1 to smaller or subtracting 1 from the larger number as in this case.)
b) Square the mean = 26^2 = 676
c) Subtract 1 from the last result = 676 − 1 = 675
Hence, 25 × 27 = 675

Example:– Multiply 74 by 76

Solution:– a) Mean = (74 + 76)/ 2 = 75. (Mean can be found by adding 1 to smaller or subtracting 1 from the larger number in this case.)

b) Square the mean = 75^2 = 5625
c) Subtract 1 from the last result = 5625 − 1 = 5624
Hence, 74 × 76 = 5624

Example:− Multiply 82 by 84

Solution:− a) Mean = (82 + 84)/ 2 = 83. (Mean can be found by adding 1 to the smaller or subtracting 1 from the larger number as in this case.)
b) Square the mean = 83^2 = 6889
c) Subtract 1 from the last result = 6889 − 1 = 6888

5. When the difference between the digits to be multiplied is 3

Rule:− a) Add 1 to the smaller number and square it
b) Subtract 1 from the smaller number and add to the previous result

Example:− Multiply 28 by 31

Solution:− Here the smaller number is 28.
a) Add 1 to it = 28 + 1 = 29
b) Square it = 29^2 = 841
c) Subtract 1 from the smaller number and add to the previous result = 841 + 28 − 1 = 868
Hence, 28 × 31 = 868

Example:− Multiply 24 by 27

Solution:− Here the smaller number is 24.
a) Add 1 to it = 24 + 1 = 25
b) Square it = 25^2 = 625
c) Subtract 1 from the smaller number and add to the previous result = 625 + 24 − 1 = 648
Hence, 24 × 27 = 648

Example:– Multiply 95 by 98

Solution:– Here the smaller number is 95.
  a) Add 1 to it = 95 + 1 = 96
  b) Square it = 96^2 = 9216
  c) Subtract 1 from the smaller number and add to the previous result = 9216 + 95 – 1 = 9310
  Hence, 95 × 98 = 9310

6. When the difference between the two numbers to be multiplied is 4

Rule:– a) Take the mean of numbers. If the numbers are a and b, where a >b, then mean is either a – 2 or b + 2
  b) Take the square of mean number.
  c) Subtract 4 from the result.

Example:– Multiply 65 by 69

Solution:– Here the difference between the numbers to be multiplied is 4. Take its mean.
  a) Mean = 65 + 2 = 67
  b) Square it = 67^2 = 4489
  c) Subtract 4 from the previous result = 4489 – 4 = 4485
  Hence, 65 × 69 = 4485

Example:– Multiply 84 by 88

Solution:– Here the difference between the numbers to be multiplied is 4. Take its mean.
  a) Mean = 84 + 2 = 86
  b) Square it = 86^2 = 7396
  c) Subtract 4 from the previous result = 7396 – 4 = 7392
  Hence, 84 × 88 = 7392

Example:– Multiply 42 by 46

Solution:– Here the difference between the numbers to be multiplied is 4. Take its mean.
  a) Mean = 42 + 2 = 44
  b) Square it = 44^2 = 1936
  c) Subtract 4 from the previous result = 1936 − 4 = 1932
  Hence, 42 × 46 = 1932

7. When the difference between the two numbers to be multiplied is 6

Rule:– a) Take the mean of numbers.
  b) Take the square of mean number.
  c) Subtract 9 from the result.

Example:– Multiply 42 by 48

Solution:– Here the difference between the numbers to be multiplied is 6. Take its mean.
  a) Mean = 42 + 3 = 45
  b) Square it = 45^2 = 2025
  c) Subtract 9 from the previous result = 2025 − 9 = 2016
  Hence, 42 × 48 = 2016

Example:– Multiply 67 by 61

Solution:– Here the difference between the numbers to be multiplied is 6. Take its mean.
  a) Mean = (61 + 67)/2 = 64
  b) Square it = 64^2 = 4096
  c) Subtract 9 from the previous result = 4096 − 9 = 4087
  Hence, 67 × 61 = 4087

Example:– Multiply 73 by 79

Solution:– Here the difference between the numbers to be multiplied is 6. Take its mean.
  a) Mean = 73 + 3 = 76
  b) Square it = 76^2 = 5776
  c) Subtract 9 from the previous result = 5776 – 9 = 5767
  Hence, 73 × 79 = 5767

8. When the difference between the two numbers to be multiplied is 8

Rule:– a) Take the mean of numbers. If the numbers are a and b; where a >b then mean is either a – 4 or b + 4
  b) Take the square of mean number.
  c) Subtract 16 from the result.

Example:– Multiply 64 by 72

Solution:– Here the difference between the numbers to be multiplied is 8. Take its mean.
  a) Mean = 64 + 4 = 68
  b) Square it = 68^2 = 4624
  c) Subtract 16 from the previous result = 4624 – 16 = 4608
  Hence, 64 × 72 = 4608

Example:– Multiply 41 by 49

Solution:– a) Mean = 41 + 4 = 45
  b) Square it = 45^2 = 2025
  c) Subtract 16 from the previous result = 2025 –16 = 2009
  Hence, 41 × 49 = 2009

Example:– Multiply 35 by 43

Solution:- a) Mean = 35 + 4 = 39
b) Square it = 39^2 = 1521
c) Subtract 16 from the previous result = 1521 − 16 = 1505
Hence, 35 × 43 = 1505

9. When the difference between the two numbers to be multiplied is 10

Rule:- a) Take the mean of numbers. If the numbers are a and b; where a >b then mean is either a − 5 or b + 5
b) Take the square of mean number.
c) Subtract 25 from the result.

Example:- Multiply 84 by 94

Solution:- Here the difference between the numbers to be multiplied is 10. Take its mean.
a) Mean = 84 + 5 = 89
b) Square it = 89^2 = 7921
c) Subtract 25 from the previous result = 7921 − 25 = 7896
Hence, 84 × 94 = 7896

Example:- Multiply 66 by 76

Solution:- a) Mean = 66 + 5 = 71
b) Square it = 71^2 = 5041
c) Subtract 25 from the previous result = 5041 − 25 = 5016
Hence, 66 × 76 = 5016

Example:- Multiply 25 by 35

Solution:- a) Mean = 25 + 5 = 30
b) Square it = 30^2 = 900
c) Subtract 25 from the previous result = 900 − 25

$$= 875$$
Hence, $25 \times 35 = 875$

10. Multiplication by 11

Multiplication of any number by 11 can be done orally in a single line. Once the technique for multiplication of a number with 11 is mastered, it can be further extended for numbers such as 22, 33, 44, etc. by simply splitting the multiplicand as 11×2, 11×3 or 11×4. In mensuration, when you need to calculate the volume and surface area of three-dimensional objects such as cylinder, sphere, cone, pyramid, frustum etc. you need to multiply the number by 22 ($\pi = 22/7$). This method will help you immensely there.

Rule:−
- Place the number to be multiplied by 11 in a bracket and put zeros on either side.
- Start adding the two numbers at a time from right to left. If the sum of two numbers in any case exceeds 10, the digit at the tenth place shall be carried over to the next sum, as is usually done in simple addition.

Example:− Multiply 3251 by 11

Solution:−

Place the number in a bracket and put zeros on either side.

$$0 \; (\; 3 \; 2 \; 5 \; 1 \;) \; 0$$

Add the digit from right to left as shown above.

$0 + 3 \;|\; 3 + 2 \;|\; 2 + 5 \;|\; 5 + 1 \;|\; 1 + 0$
$= 3\;5\;7\;6\;1$
Hence $3251 \times 11 = 35761$

Example:– Multiply 4876254 by 11

Solution:–

Place the number in a bracket and put zeros on either side.

0(4 8 7 6 2 5 4)0

Add the digit from right to left as shown above.

= 0+4| 4+8 | 8+7 | 7+6 | 6+2 | 2+5 | 5+4 | 4+0

= 4 | 12 | 15 | 13 | 8 | 7 | 9 | 4

= 4 | 12 | 16 | 3 | 8 | 7 | 9 | 4

= 4 | 13 | 6 | 3 | 8 | 7 | 9 | 4

= 5 3 6 3 8 7 9 4

Hence, 4876254 × 11 = 53638794

There is no need to write so many steps for this multiplication. The break-up shown here is only to make you understand each and every step on your own. I know once you start practising solving bigger numbers you will have some hiccups initially, but later you will know the answer in the first look next time.

11. Multiplication by 12

Rule:– The whole operation is similar to that of multiplication by 11 done above with a little difference that here you will start multiplying the digit in brackets one by one by 2 and add the next succeeding digit.

Let's see how it works for a better understanding.

Example:– Multiply 13 by 12

Solution:– a) Put the multiplicand 13 inside a bracket placing one zero on either side.
0{13}0

b) Multiply the unit digit 3 by 2 and add the 0 to it
   $3 \times 2 + 0 = 6$
c) Multiply the ten's digit 1 by 2 and add 3 to the next succeeding digit to it
   $1 \times 2 + 3 = 5$
d) Multiply the last 0 (zero) by 2 and add 1 to it
   $0 \times 2 + 1 = 1$
   Hence, $13 \times 12 = 156$

It is clear from the above example that we should start from the unit digit and keep the left zero for the end.

Example:– Multiply 247 by 12

Solution:–
a) Put the multiplicand 247 inside a bracket placing one zero on either side.
   0 {247} 0
b) Multiply the unit digit 7 by 2 and add the 0 to it
   $7 \times 2 + 0 = 14$
c) Multiply the ten's digit 4 by 2 and add 7 to the next succeeding digit to it
   $4 \times 2 + 7 = 15$
d) Multiply the digit at hundred place (2) by 2 and add 4 to its succeeding digit.
   $2 \times 2 + 4 = 8$
d) Multiply the last 0 (zero) by 2 and add 2 to it
   $0 \times 2 + 2 = 2$

The whole operation can be done in one line as shown here.

$0 \times 2 + 2 / 2 \times 2 + 4 / 4 \times 2 + 7 / 7 \times 2 + 0$
$= 2 / 8 / 15 / 14$
$= 2964$
Hence, $247 \times 12 = 2964$

Example:– Multiply 301247 by 12

Solution:– a) Put the multiplicand 247 inside a bracket placing one zero on either side.
0 {301247} 0

b) Multiply the unit digit 7 by 2 and add the 0 to it
$7 \times 2 + 0 = 14$

c) Multiply the ten's digit 4 by 2 and add 7 to the next succeeding digit to it
$4 \times 2 + 7 = 15$

d) Multiply the digit at hundred place (2) by 2 and add 4 to its succeeding digit.
$2 \times 2 + 4 = 8$

e) Multiply the digit at thousand place (1) by 2 and add 2 to its succeeding digit.
$1 \times 2 + 2 = 4$

f) Multiply 0 by 2 and add 1 to its succeeding digit.
$0 \times 2 + 1 = 1$

g) Multiply 3 by 2 and add 0 to its succeeding digit.
$3 \times 2 + 0 = 6$

d) Multiply the last 0 (zero) by 2 and add 3 to it
$0 \times 2 + 3 = 3$

The whole operation can be done in one line as shown here.

$0 \times 2 + 3 / 3 \times 2 + 0 / 0 \times 2 + 1 / 1 \times 2 + 2 / 2 \times 2 + 4 / 4 \times 2 + 7 / 7 \times 2 + 0$

= 3/ 6 / 1/ 4 / 8 / 15 / 14
= 3614964

Hence, 301247 × 12 = 3614964

Multiplication by 13 and 14 can be carried out in the same fashion with only difference—instead of multiplying by 2 you have to multiply by 3 and 4 respectively. The rest of the process is the same. I am giving one more example for you and then you can do some examples on your own.

Example:– Multiply 141 by 13

Solution:– a) Put the multiplicand 141 inside a bracket placing one zero on either side.
0 {141}0
b) Multiply the unit digit 1 by 3 and add the 0 to it
$1 \times 3 + 0 = 3$
c) Multiply the ten's digit 4 by 3 and add 1 to the next succeeding digit to it
$4 \times 3 + 1 = 13$
d) Multiply the hundred digit 1 by 3 and add 4 to the next succeeding digit to it
$1 \times 3 + 4 = 7$
d) Multiply the last 0 (zero) by 3 and add 1 to it

$0 \times 3 + 1 = 1$

The whole operation can be done in one line as shown here.
$0 \times 3 + 1 / 1 \times 3 + 4 / 4 \times 3 + 1 / 1 \times 3 + 0$
$= 1 / 7 / 13 / 3$
$= 1833$

Hence, $141 \times 13 = 1833$

12. Multiplication by 15

Multiplication of any number by 15 can be done by the previous method but I shall make some changes to it and make you learn another method which is better than the previous one.

Rule:– a) Put a zero at the end of the multiplicand.
b) Divide the previous result by 2
c) Add both the results

Example:– Multiply 24 by 15

Solution:– a) Put one zero at the end of 24 = 240
b) Divide it by 2 = 240 ÷ 2 = 120

c) Add the previous two result = 240 + 120 = 360
   Hence, 24 × 15 = 360

Example:– Multiply 36 by 15

Solution:– a) Put one zero at the end of 36 = 360
   b) Divide it by 2 = 360 ÷ 2 = 180
   c) Add the previous two results = 360 + 180 = 540
   Hence, 36 × 15 = 540

Example:– Multiply 2462 by 15

Solution:– a) Put one zero at the end of 2462 = 24620
   b) Divide it by 2 = 24620 ÷ 2 = 12310
   c) Add the previous two results = 24620 + 12310 = 36930
   Hence, 2462 × 15 = 36930

13. Multiplication by 18

Multiplication of 18 can be done easily if you do the multiplication in breaks. We all know that multiplication of any number by 10 or its multiple is child's play. We shall apply the same trick here. 20 = 18 + 2 or 20 – 2 = 18. Let's look at the method before I take an example to make clear the modus operandi of it.

   a) Multiply the number by 2
   b) Put one zero at the end of the results obtained
   c) Take the difference of both the results and you get the answer

Example:– 42 × 18 = ?

Solution:–

   a) Multiply the number by 2 = 42 × 2 = 84
   b) Put one zero at the end of the result obtained = 840

    c) Take the difference of both the results and you get the answer = 840 − 84 = 756
    Hence, 42 × 18 = 756

Example:– 94 × 18 = ?

Solution:–

    a) Multiply the number by 2 = 94 × 2 = 188
    b) Put one zero at the end of the result obtained = 1880
    c) Take the difference of both the results and you get the answer = 1880 − 188 = 1692
    Hence, 94 × 18 = 1692

Example:– 4352 × 18 = ?

Solution:–

    a) Multiply the number by 2 = 4352 × 2 = 8704
    b) Put one zero at the end of the result obtained = 87040
    c) Take the difference of both the results and you get the answer = 87040 − 8704 = 78336
    Hence, 4352 × 18 = 78336

14. Multiplication by 25

Rule:– If I ask a class 1 student to multiply a number by 100, there is a higher probability that he will come out with correct answer. This is due to the fact that multiplying a number by 10, 100, 1000, etc. is so simple that it can be done mentally in no time. The present method of multiplying a number by 25 is simply based on this technique.

When you are multiplying a number by 25, put two zeros (00) to the right of the multiplicand and divide it by 4.

Example:– Multiply 164 by 25

Solution:– Put two zeros to the right of 164, i.e. 16400
   Divide it by 4 = 16400 / 4 = 4100
   Hence, 25 × 164 = 4100

Example:– Multiply 98 by 25

Solution:– Put two zeros to the right making it 9800
   Divide it by 4, 9800 / 4 = 2450
   98 × 25 = 2450

Example:– Multiply 428764 by 25

Solution:– Put two zeros to the right of 428764, i.e. 42876400
   Divide it by 4 = 42876400 / 4 = 10719100
   428764 × 25 = 10719100

15. Multiply by 50

Rule:– Put two zeros to the right of the number to be multiplied and divide it by 2.

Example:– Multiply 47 by 50

Solution:– Place 2 zeros after 47, making it 4700
   Divide it by 2 = 4700/2 = 2350
   Hence, 47 × 50 = 2350

Example:– Multiply 62876 by 50

Solution:– Place 2 zeros after 62876, making it 6287600
   Divide it by 2 = 6287600/2 = 3143800
   Hence, 62876 × 50 = 3143800

Example:– Multiply 246893 by 50

Solution:– Place 2 zeros after 246893, making it 24689300
   Divide it by 2 = 24689300/2 = 12344600
   Hence, 246893 × 50 = 12344600

16. Multiplication by 51

Multiplication by 51 can be fun and easy too! It has two parts. In the left part write the number divided by 2 whereas in the right part just copy the multiplicand and the answer is yours. In case the left hand part has a mixed fraction involving ½, keep the whole part as usual and transfer the ½ = 50 to the right side and add it.

Example:– 48 × 51 = ?

Solution:– The answer will have two parts —/—
        a) Place the number to be multiplied at the right side: —/ 48
        b) Divide the multiplicand by 2 and keep it to the left: 48 ÷ 2 / 48 = 24 / 48
        Hence, 48 × 51 = 2448

Example:– 125 × 51 = ?

Solution:– The answer will have two parts —/—
        a) Place the number to be multiplied at the right side: —/ 125
        b) Divide the multiplicand by 2 and keep it to the left: 125 ÷ 2 /125 = 62½ / 125
        = 62 / 50 + 125
        = 62 / 175
        = 6375
        Hence, 125 × 51 = 6375

Example:– 87025 × 51 = ?

Solution:– The answer will have two parts —/—
        a) Place the number to be multiplied at the right side: —/ 87025
        b) Divide the multiplicand by 2 and keep it to the left: 87025 ÷ 2 /87025

$$= 43512½ / 87025$$
$$= 43512 / 50 + 87025$$
$$= 43512 / 87075$$
$$= 44382/75$$
Hence, $87025 \times 51 = 4438275$

17. Multiplication by 125

When you are multiplying a number by 125, put three zeros (000) to the right of the multiplicand and divide it by 8.

Example:– Multiply 164 by 125

Solution:– Put 3 zeros to the right of 164, i.e. 164000
Divide it by $8 = 164000 / 8 = 20500$
Hence, $125 \times 164 = 20500$

Example:– Multiply 987 by 125

Solution:– Put 3 zeros to the right, making it 987000
Divide it by $8 = 987000 / 8 = 123500$
Hence, $987 \times 125 = 123500$

Example:– Multiply 428764 by 125

Solution:– Put 3 zeros to the right of $428764 = 428764000$
Divide it by $8 = 428764000 / 8 = 53595500$
Hence, $428764 \times 125 = 53595500$

18. Multiplication by recurrence of 9s

Multiplication of numbers with a recurrence of 9s is child's play provided:–

a) the number of digits in the multiplicand and number of 9s in the multiplier is same
b) or, the number of 9s in the multiplier are more than that of digits in the multiplicand

In both of the above situations you have to subtract 1 from the multiplicand and keep it at the left side. This result placed in the left side will be further subtracted from the 9s in the multipliers.

Example:– 4569 × 9999

Solution:– a) Subtract 1 from the multiplicand = 4569 – 1 = 4568
b) Subtract the result from the recurrence of 9's, i.e. 9999 = 9999 – 4568 = 5431
Combine both the result to obtain the answer.
Hence, 4569 × 9999 = 45685431

Example:– Multiply 89654876 by 99999999

Solution:–
LHS = 89654876 – 1 = 89654875
RHS = 99999999 – 89654875 = 10345124
Hence, 89654876 × 99999999 = 8965487510345124

Example:– Multiply 83465087629 by 99999999999

Solution:–
LHS = 83465087629 – 1 = 83465087628
RHS = 99999999999 – 83465087628 = 16534912371
Hence, 83465087629 × 99999999999 = 8346508762816534912371

Hope you have enjoyed the journey of multiplication tricks very much. Such tricks and many more let you do your calculation faster than the normal method with absolutely no chance of mistake. For better practice, take at least five examples of each type and practise them.

5

Division Without Dilemma

Division is the process of finding how many times a number is contained in another. It is a rapid way of subtracting. It is the reverse of multiplication just as subtraction is the reverse of addition.

If we say 12 ÷ 3 = 4, it means 3 × 4 = 12.

In the process of division, the number which is to be divided is called Dividend and the number by which we divide the dividend is called Divisor. There is another term Quotient which tells us how many times the divisor can divide the dividend. Remainder is the number obtained after subtracting the product of divisor and quotient from the dividend.

$$\begin{array}{r}\text{Dividend}\\ \text{Divisor } 6\overline{)45}\,(7 \quad \text{Quotient}\\ -42\\ \hline 3 \text{ Remainder}\end{array}$$

There is a famous formula which you must be aware of since your schooldays and which is very helpful in checking the division.

Dividend = Divisor × Quotient + Remainder

When any dividend is fully divided by a divisor leaving 0 as remainder we say the dividend is fully divisible. In order to understand division you should first memorize the divisibility rule of numbers. In the present chapter we shall focus on the **divisibility rule** of numbers apart from some shortcut rules to divide a number.

Divisibility Rules of Numbers

Divisibility by 2:– Any number that ends with 0, 2, 4, 6 or 8 is divisible by 2.

Example:– 4627890, 598, 29856, 8880996774

Divisibility by 3:– If the sum of all digits of the number is divisible by 3, the number is divisible by 3.

Example:– 24638124 is divisible by 3 as $2 + 4 + 6 + 3 + 8 + 1 + 2 + 4 = 30$ is divisible by 3

Divisibility by 4:– If any number ends with 00 or its last two digits (unit and tens) is divisible by 4 then the whole number is divisible by 4.

Example:– 245552 is divisible by 4 as its last two digits 52 is divisible by 4.

65298700 is divisible by 4 as the number ends with 00.

Divisibility by 5:– A number is divisible by 5 if its unit digit is either 0 or 5.

Example:– 19997665, 654298760

Divisibility by 6:– If a number is divisible by 2 and 3 separately then the number is divisible by 6.

Example:– 25134 is divisible by 2 as it ends with 4, moreover $2 + 5 + 1 + 3 + 4 = 15$ is also divisible by 3 hence 25134 is divisible by 6.

Divisibility by 7:– Divisibility of a number by 7 is not that easy but you can use this method to check divisibility. However, it needs a little practice. Take the number and multiply each digit beginning on the right hand side (ones) by 1, 3, 2, 6, 4, 5. Repeat this sequence if necessary. Add the product. If the sum is divisible by 7, the number will be divisible by 7.

Example:– Check whether 2016 is divisible by 7

6(1) + 1(3) + 0(2) + 2(6) = 21 is divisible by 7 hence 2016 is divisible by 7.

Divisibility by 8:– A number is divisible by 8 if it ends with 000 or the last three digits of the number to be divided is divisible by 8.

Example:– 7000, 70008

Divisibility by 9:– A number is divisible by 8 if the sum of digits is divisible by 9.

Example:– 54387531 is divisible by 9 because 5 + 4 + 3 + 8 + 7 + 5 + 3 + 1 = 36 is divisible by 9.

Divisibility by 10:– A number is divisible by 10 if it ends with 0.

Example:– 24567890 is divisible by 10

Divisibility by 11:– A number is divisible by 11 if the difference between the sum of the digits at odd places and the sum of digits at the even places is either zero or a number divisible by 11.

Example:– Check whether 584397 is divisible by 11

7 + 3 + 8 = 18 = Sum of odd position digits

9 + 4 + 5 = 18 = Sum of even position digits.

18 – 18 = 0 = Difference between sum of odd and even places.

Hence, 584397 is divisible by 11

Shortcut Method of Division

a) Division by 10, 100, 1000, etc.:– Separate 1, 2, 3, 4 digits respectively from the right. The number formed by the left digit is the quotient and number formed by the right digits is the remainder.

Example:— a) $123 \div 10 = 12.3$
b) $564321 \div 1000 = 564.321$
c) $78654 \div 100 = 786.54$
d) $344678 \div 1000000 = 0.344678$

b) Division by 5:— Division by 5 is simple—merely multiply numerator by 2 and divide the product obtained by 10.

Example:— Divide 65432 by 5

Solution:— $65432 \div 5 = (65432 \times 2) \div 10 = 130864 \div 10 = 13086.4$

Example:— Divide 1234 by 5

Solution:— $1234 \div 5 = (1234 \times 2) \div 10 = 2468 \div 10 = 246.8$

c) Division by 25:— Remember the multiplication of a number by 25? Division of a number by 25 also works on the same principle. Multiply the dividend by 4 and move decimal two places left which will give you the correct answer.

Example:— $641 \div 25 = ?$

Solution:— Multiply 641 by 4 = $641 \times 4 = 2564$

Multiplication of any number by 4 can be done in breaks. First multiply the number by 2 and then multiply the product again by 2. It works better.

$641 \times 2 = 1200 + 82 = 1282$

$1282 \times 2 = 1200 \times 2 + 80 \times 2 + 2 \times 2 = 2400 + 160 + 4 = 2564$

Now move decimal places 2 digits left = 25.64

Hence, $641 \div 25 = 25.64$

Example:— $12652 \div 25 = ?$

Solution:— $12652 \times 4 = 12000 \times 4 + 600 \times 4 + 50 \times 4 + 2 \times 4$
$= 48000 + 2400 + 200 + 8 = 50608$

Move decimal point 2 digits left = 506.08

d) Division by 35:- A number of 2 – 3 digits can be divided by 35 by simply multiplying the number by 2 and dividing the result by 7. Finally move the decimal one place to the left.

Example:- 61 ÷ 35 =?

Solution:- Multiply 61 by 2 = 61 × 2 = 122
Divide it by 7 = 122 ÷ 7 = 17.428...
Move decimal one point left = 1.7428...

Example:- 4521 ÷ 35 = ?

Solution:- Multiply 4521 by 2 = 4521 × 2 = 9042
Divide it by 7 = 9042 ÷ 7 = 1291.71428...
Move decimal one point left = 1291.71428...

e) Division by 40: If you are dividing a 2 – 3 digit number by 40; multiply it by 5 and divide the product by 2. Now you are about to reach the answer. Move decimal places to two points left and you have reached your answer.

Example:- 21 ÷ 40 = ?

Solution:- Multiply by 5 = 21 × 5 = 105
Divide by 2 = 105 ÷ 2 = 52.5
Move decimal to two points left = 0.525
Hence, 21 ÷ 40 = 0.525

Example:- 1562 ÷ 40 = ?

Solution:- Multiply by 5 = 1562 × 5 = 7810
Divide by 2 = 7810 ÷ 2 = 3905
Move decimal to two points left = 39.05
Hence, 1562 ÷ 40 = 39.05

f) Division by 15:- If you want to divide any number by 15 follow these simple steps:-
  i) Multiply the number by 2
  ii) Divide the product by 3

iii) Move the decimal to one point left

Example:– $68 \div 15 =$?

Solution:– Multiply 68 by 2 = 68 × 2 = 136
Divide by 3 = 136 ÷ 3 = 45.33
Move decimal to one point left = 4.533

Example:– $6248 \div 15 =$?

Solution:– Multiply 6248 by 2 = 6248 × 2 = 12496
Divide by 3 = 12496 ÷ 3 = 4165.33
Move decimal to one point left = 416.533

g) Division by 0.125:– Select the number which you are dividing by 0.125. Multiply it by 8 and you get the answer.

Example:– $21 \div 0.125 =$?

Solution:– Multiply 21 by 8 = 21 × 8 = 168
Hence, 21 ÷ 0.125 = 168

Example:– $6542 \div 0.125 =$?

Solution:– Multiply 6542 by 8 = 6542 × 8 = 52336
Hence, 6542 ÷ 0.125 = 52336

h) Division by 50:– Division by 50 is easy to execute. Simply multiply the number by 2 and move decimal two points left.

Example:– $187654 \div 50 =$?

Solution:– Multiply 187654 by 2 = 187654 × 2 = 375308
Move decimal two points left = 3753.08

Example:– $654 \div 50 =$?

Solution:– Multiply 654 by 2 = 654 × 2 = 1308
Move decimal two points left = 13.08

i) Division by 75:– In order to divide a number by 75, multiply the number by 4 and divide the product by 3. To get the final result move the decimal to two points on the left.

Example:— 154 ÷ 75 = ?

Solution:— Multiply 154 by 4 = 154 × 4 = 616
Divide the number by 3 = 616 ÷ 3 = 205.33
Move the decimal two points to left = 2.0533

Example:— 4862 ÷ 75 = ?

Solution:— Multiply 4862 by 4 = 4862 × 4 = 19448
Divide the number by 3 = 19448 ÷ 3 = 6482.66
Move the decimal two points to the left = 64.8266

j) Division by 125:— Division by 125 is child's play; if you multiply the number by 8 and move the decimal three places to the left you will have your answer.

Example:— 54 ÷ 125 = ?

Solution:— Multiply 54 by 8 = 54 × 8 = 432
Move the decimal three points to the left = 0.432

Example:— 420 ÷ 125 =?

Solution:— Multiply 420 by 8 = 420 × 8 = 3360
Move the decimal three points to the left = 3.360

Some Interesting Patterns on Division of 9, 99,999, etc.

In multiplication you have seen how simple it is to multiply a number with 9, 99, 999.... Division of a number with 9 or its recurring digits is also very interesting. Let's play a magical game.

$$12345679 \times 9 = 111,111,111$$
$$12345679 \times 18 = 222,222,222$$
$$12345679 \times 27 = 333,333,333$$
$$12345679 \times 36 = 444,444,444$$

$$12345679 \times 45 = 555{,}555{,}555$$
$$12345679 \times 54 = 666{,}666{,}666$$
$$12345679 \times 63 = 777{,}777{,}777$$
$$12345679 \times 72 = 888{,}888{,}888$$
$$12345679 \times 81 = 999{,}999{,}999$$

Does it look like a puzzle? Let's learn one more interesting puzzle of 9 before I return to the main topic.

$1 \div 9 = 0.111111...$ $\qquad 2 \div 9 = 0.222222...$
$3 \div 9 = 0.333333...$ $\qquad 4 \div 9 = 0.444444...$
$5 \div 9 = 0.555555...$ $\qquad 6 \div 9 = 0.666666...$
$7 \div 9 = 0.777777...$ $\qquad 8 \div 9 = 0.888888...$

Let's return to the topic of division. Now we shall learn the different methods of division by 9.

Dividing a Two-Digit Number by 9

Divide the dividend into two parts. The left part gives you the quotient and the right part gives you the remainder.

If $a\,b \div 9$ then Quotient = **a** and Remainder = **a + b**; provided **a + b** < 9. In case **a + b** ≥ 9 add 1 to the quotient and remainder in this case will be **a + b − 9**.

Example:– $12 \div 9 = ?$

Solution:– Quotient = 1 / Remainder = 1 + 2 = 3

Example:– $52 \div 9 = ?$

Solution:– Quotient = 5 / Remainder = 5 + 2 = 7

Example:– $98 \div 9 = ?$

Solution:– Quotient = 9 / Remainder = 9 + 8 = 17 > 9. Hence Final quotient = 9 + 1 = 10 and Remainder = 17 − 9 = 8

Example:– $19 \div 9 = ?$

Solution:– Quotient = 1 / Remainder = 1 + 9 = 10. Hence Final quotient = 1 + 1 = 2 and Remainder = 10 – 9 = 1

Dividing a Three-Digit Number by 9

Suppose you are dividing a three-digit number by 9 and you want to get the answer instantly then this method will help you a lot.

a b c ÷ 9; Quotient = a / b + a and Remainder = a + b + c

For your own convenience you could add the digits from left, one by one, and the sum of all the three digits is your remainder and the numbers arranged previous to the remainder is the quotient.

For a b c ÷ 9 Add the numbers from left which is: a / a + b / a + b + c.

Hence the quotient = a / a + b and Remainder = a + b + c

Example:– 103 ÷ 9 = ?

Solution:– First divide 103 into two parts the second part should consist of as many numbers as the number of 9s. Add the left part to get the quotient and the sum of each digit on the left and right part gives you the remainder.

Quotient = 1 / 1 + 0 = 11
Remainder = 1 + 0 + 3 = 4

Example:– 343 ÷ 9 = ?

Solution:– First divide 343 into two parts. The second part should consist of as many numbers as the number of 9s. Add the left part to get the quotient and the sum of each digit on the left and right part gives you the remainder.

Quotient = 3 / 3 + 4 = 37
Remainder = 3 + 4 + 3 = 10 > 9

Hence Final Quotient = 37 + 1 = 38 and Remainder = 10 – 9 = 1

Division of a Number With More Than 3 Digits

Division of a number having more than 3 digits will follow the same instructional method as mentioned above.

Example:– 1023425 ÷ 9 = ?

Solution:– First divide 1023425 into two parts, the second part will have only one digit as there is only one 9 in the divisor. Add the left part to get the quotient and the sum of each digit on the left and right part gives you the remainder.

Quotient = 1 / 1 + 0 / 1+0 + 2/ 1+0 + 2 + 3/ / 1+0 + 2 + 3 + 4 / 1+0 + 2 + 3 + 4 +2

= 1136/$_1$0 /$_1$2 = 113712

Remainder = 1 + 0 + 2 + 3 + 4 + 2 + 5 = 17 > 9

Hence final quotient = 113712 + 1 = 113713 and remainder = 17 – 9 = 8

Example:– 3425 ÷ 9 = ?

Solution:– First divide 3425 into two parts, the second part will have only one digit as there is only one 9 in the divisor. Add the left part to get the quotient and sum of each digit on the left and right part gives you the remainder.

Quotient = 3 / 3 + 4 / 3+ 4 + 2 = 379

Remainder = 3 + 4 + 2 + 5 = 14 > 9

Hence final quotient = 379 + 1 = 380 and remainder = 14 – 9 = 5

Hope you have enjoyed the journey of division. For more detailed information on division you can read *The Essentials of Vedic Mathematics* and try out the Vedic Technique of Division.

6

Square: Child's Play

Introduction

The square of a number is that number multiplied by itself. The Greeks were the first to form different numerical patterns using pebbles. They arranged the pebbles in the shapes of a triangle, square, pyramid, pentagon, and hexagon. A good way to visualize this is, if you have a square made of bricks in your garden and you want to know the total number of bricks making up the square, you count the number of bricks on one side and multiply the number by itself to get answer. Here are few square arrangements shown.

$$1 \quad 2\times2 \quad 3\times3 \quad 4\times4 \quad 5\times5$$

The above shapes of pebbles form a pattern of square numbers. In the language of indices:

$A \times A = A^2$
$4 \times 4 = 4^2$

An Interesting Pattern

$1 = 1 = 1^2$

$1 + 3 = 4 = 2^2$
$1 + 3 + 5 = 9 = 3^2$
$1 + 3 + 5 + 7 = 16 = 4^2$
$1 + 3 + 5 + 7 + 9 = 25 = 5^2$
$1 + 3 + 5 + 7 + 9 + 11 = 36 = 6^2$
$1 + 3 + 5 + 7 + 9 + 11 + 13 = 49 = 7^2$
$1 + 3 + 5 + 7 + 9 + 11 + 13 + 15 = 64 = 8^2$
$1 + 3 + 5 + 7 + 9 + 11 + 13 + 15 + 17 = 81 = 9^2$
$1 + 3 + 5 + 7 + 9 + 11 + 13 + 15 + 17 + 19 = 100 = 10^2$

This pattern shows that the sum of n odd numbers.

$$1 + 3 + 5 + \text{------} + 2n - 1 = n^2$$

I have used the pebbles arrangement to show how the above odd number series are formed.

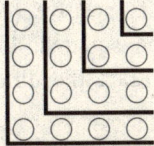

This is a 4 × 4 square. Each higher square number is formed by adding an L-shaped set of pebbles.

$1 + 3 = 4$

$1 + 3 + 5 = 9$ and so on.

As far as squaring a number is concerned there are several methods which will help you find the answer in seconds. I will try to open up the methods one by one in order of their complexity.

I have divided this chapter into two parts:–

1. Squaring near base number
2. Special method to find the square number

The first part is easy as you hardly need to memorize anything and understanding this part is important as you can base it on other such types of squaring methods.

Squaring near Base Number

In multiplication we have discussed in detail the base number. A base number is in the form of 10^n. In other words, if you find a number near base 10, 100, 1000...etc. you can do the squaring of such numbers quite comfortably.

Squaring a Number near Base 10, 100, 1000, etc.

Finding the square of a number which is near the base 10, 100, 1000... is an easy task and can be done mentally in no time with a little practice. Follow the steps carefully.

a) Estimate the difference between the number to be squared from the base 10, 100, 1000...
b) If the difference is positive (+) add the difference to the number to be squared. In case the difference is negative (−), subtract the difference from the number to be squared.
c) Square the difference and place it right. The number of digits on the right side will depend upon the number of zeros in the base. For the base 10, the number of digits on the right should be 1 whereas for the base 100, the number of digits on the right will be 2. In case there are more digits on the right side, add the extreme left digit of the right side to the number on the left side.

Example:− Find the square of 12

Solution:− Base = 10
Difference = 12 − 10 = + 2
$(12)^2 = 12 + 2 / 2^2 = 144$

Example:– Find the square of 15

Solution:– Base = 10
Difference = 15 − 10 = +5
$(15)^2 = 15 + 5 / 5^2 = 20 / 25 = 225$

Example:– Find the square of 94

Solution:– Base = 100
Difference = 94 − 100 = −6
$(94)^2 = 94-6 / (-6)^2 = 88 / 36 = 8836$

(Since our base is 100 there should be 2 digits at the right side)

Example:– Find the square of 108

Solution:– Base = 100
Difference = 108 − 100 = 8
$(108)^2 = 108 + 8 / (8)^2 = 116 / 64 = 11664$

Example:– Find the square of 98

Solution:– Base = 100
Difference = 98 − 100 = −2
$(98)^2 = 98-2 / (-2)^2 = 96 / 04 = 9604$

(Since our base is 100 there should be 2 digits on the right side. Hence 4 on the right side is written as 04)

Example:– Find the square of 994

Solution:– Base = 1000
Difference = 994 − 1000 = −6
$(994)^2 = 994-6 / (-6)^2 = 988 / 036 = 988036$

(Since our base is 1000 so there should be 3 digits at the right side. Hence 36 is written as 036)

Squaring a Number near Base 20, 200, 2000...

Squaring a number near base 20, 200, 2000... can be solved by merely changing the base number in the multiple of 10, 100, 1000....

The whole operation of squaring such numbers will be the same with the only difference that the left part of the solution will be multiplied by 2.

$20 = 2 \times 10 \quad 200 = 2 \times 100 \quad 2000 = 2 \times 1000$ etc.

Example:– Find the square of 23

Solution:– Base = $20 = 2 \times 10$
Difference = $23 - 20 = +3$
$(23)^2 = (23 + 3) \times 2 / 3^2$ (The left side is multiplied by 2)
$= 26 \times 2 / 9$
$= 529$

Example:– Find the square of 28

Solution:– Base = $20 = 2 \times 10$
Difference = $28 - 20 = +8$
$(28)^2 = (28 + 8) \times 2 / 8^2$ (The left side is multiplied by 2)
$= 36 \times 2 / 64$
$= 72 / 64$
$= 784$

Example:– Find the square of 211

Solution:– Base = $200 = 2 \times 100$
Difference = $211 - 200 = +11$
$(211)^2 = (211 + 11) \times 2 / 11^2$ (The left side is multiplied by 2)
$= 222 \times 2 / 121$
$= 444 / 121$
$= 44521$

The left part is multiplied by 2 because $200 = 2 \times 100$. Moreover, as discussed in the previous method the number of digits on the right side depends upon the number of zeros in the base. So we keep 21 of 121 in the right side and the extreme left digit 1 is transferred to the left side.

Example:– Find the square of 193

Solution:– Base = 200 = 2 × 100
Difference = 193 – 200 = –7
$(193)^2$ = (193 – 7) × 2 / $(-7)^2$ (The left side is multiplied by 2)
= 186 × 2 / 49
= 372 / 49 = 37249

Squaring a Number near Base 30, 300, 3000...

Squaring a number near base 30, 300, 3000... can be solved by merely changing the base number in the multiple of 10, 100, 1000... as shown above.

The whole operation of squaring such number will be same with the only difference that the left part of the solution will be multiplied by 3.

30 = 3 × 10   300 = 3 × 100   3000 = 3 × 1000 etc.

Example:– Find the square of 32

Solution:– Base = 30 = 3 × 10
Difference = 32 – 30 = + 2
$(32)^2$ = (32 + 2) × 3 / 2^2 (The left side is multiplied by 3)
= 34 × 3 / 4
= 1024

Example:– Find the square of 28

Solution:– Base = 30 = 3 × 10
Difference = 28 – 30 = –2

$(28)^2 = (28-2) \times 3 / (-2)^2$ (The left side is multiplied by 3)
$= 26 \times 3 / 4$
$= 78/4$
$= 784$

Example:– Find the square of 291

Solution:– Base $= 300 = 3 \times 100$
Difference $= 291 - 300 = -9$
$(291)^2 = (291 - 9) \times 3 / (-9)^2$ (The left side is multiplied by 3 because $300 = 3 \times 100$)
$= 282 \times 3 / 81$
$= 846/ 81$
$= 84681$

Example:– Find the square of 313

Solution:– Base $= 300 = 3 \times 100$
Difference $= 313 - 300 = + 13$
$(313)^2 = (313 + 13) \times 3 / (13)^2$ (The left side is multiplied by 3)
$= 326 \times 3 / 13 + 3 /3^2$
$= 978 / 169$
$= 97969$

As discussed earlier the number of digits on the right side depends on the number of zeros in the base. Here base 300 has 2 zeros so the extreme 1 of 169 is transferred to the left side. Moreover, in the above example I have again explained the square of 13 by taking base 10 as discussed earlier.

Squaring a Number near Base 40, 400, 4000...

The whole operation of squaring such numbers will be the same with the only difference being that the left part of the solution will be multiplied by 4.

40 = 4 × 10   400 = 4 × 100   4000 = 4 × 1000 etc.

Example:– Find the square of 43

Solution:– Base = 40 = 4 × 10
Difference = 43 – 40 = + 3
$(43)^2$ = (43 + 3) × 4 / 3^2 (The left side is multiplied by 4)
= 46 × 4 / 9
= 1829

Example:– Find the square of 38

Solution:– Base = 40 = 4 × 10
Difference = 38 – 40 = –2
$(38)^2$ = (38–2) × 4 / $(-2)^2$ (The left side is multiplied by 3)
= 36 × 4 /4
= 144/4
= 1444

Example:– Find the square of 395

Solution:– Base = 400 = 4 × 100
Difference = 395 – 400 = –5
$(395)^2$ = (395 –5) × 4 / $(-5)^2$ (The left side is multiplied by 4 because 400 = 4 × 100)
= 390 × 4 / 25
= 1560/ 25
= 156025

Example:– Find the square of 387

Solution:– Base = 400 = 4 × 100
Difference = 387 – 400 = –13
$(387)^2$ = (387–13) × 4 / $(-13)^2$ (The left side is multiplied by 4)
= 374 × 4 / 13 + 3 /3^2

$$= 1496 / 169$$
$$= 149769$$

Squaring a Number near Base 25, 250, 2500...

Squiring a number near base 25, 250, 2500 can be done through a wise choice of base number. In the chapter on multiplication I have discussed a special method of multiplying a number by 250, where I divided the result by 4 after multiplying the whole by 100.

Let's look at the question this way.

$25 = ¼ \times 100$ $250 = ¼ \times 1000$ $2500 = ¼ \times 1000$ etc.

It means that in order to find the square of a number near base 25, 250, etc. we will basically divide the left side by 4. In case you get the result of the left side as a fraction we will add 25, 50, or 75... for the fractional part $¼, ²/_4$ or $¾$ as the case may be to get the answer quickly. Let me give some examples for you.

Example:– Find the square of 24

Solution:– Base = 25 = ¼ × 100

Difference = 24 − 25 = −1

$(24)^2 = (24−1) \times ¹/_4 / 1^2$ (The left side is multiplied by ¼)

$= ^{23}/_4 / 1$

$= 5¾ / 1$

$= 5 / 75 + 1$ ($³/_4 = 75$ is transferred to the right side)

$= 576$

Example:– Find the square of 243

Solution:– Base = 250 = ¼ × 1000

Difference = 243 − 250 = −7

$(243)^2 = (243−7) \times ¹/_4 / (−7)^2$ (The left side is multiplied by ¼)

$= ^{236}/_4 / 1$

= 59 / 49

= 59 / 049 (For base 1000, there should be 3 digits in the right side)

= 59049

Example:– Find the square of 263

Solution:– Base = 250 = ¼ × 1000

Difference = 263 – 250 = 13

$(263)^2 = (263 + 13) \times 1/4 / (13)^2$ (The left side is multiplied by ¼)

= $^{276}/_4$ / 169

= 69 / 169

= 69169 (For base 1000, there should be 3 digits in the right side)

Squaring a Number near Base 50, 500, 5000...

Squaring a number near base 50, 500, 5000 can be done with a wise choice of base number.

Let's look at the question this way.

50 = ½ × 100   500 = ½ × 1000   5000 = ½ × 10000 etc.

It means that in order to find the square of a number near base 50, 500, etc. We will basically divide the left side by 2. In case you get the result of left side in fraction we will add 50, 500... for the fractional part ½ as the case may be to get the answer quickly. Let me put some examples for you.

Example:– Find the square of 54

Solution:– Base = 50 = ½ ×100

Difference = 54 – 50 = 4

$(54)^2 = (54 +4) \times ½ / 4^2$ (The left side is multiplied by ½)

= $^{58}/_2$ / 16

= 29 /16

= 2916

Square: Child's Play

Example:– Find the square of 493

Solution:– Base = 500 = ½ × 1000

Difference = 493 − 500 = −7

$(493)^2$ = (493−7) × ½ / $(−7)^2$ (The left side is multiplied by ½)

= $^{486}/_2$ /49

= 243 / 49

= 243 /049 (For base 1000, there should be 3 digits in the right side)

= 243049

Example:– Find the square of 513

Solution:– Base = 500 = ½ ×1000

Difference = 513 − 500 = 13

$(513)^2$ = (513+ 13) × ½ / $(13)^2$ (The left side is multiplied by ½)

= $^{526}/_2$ /169

= 263 / 169

= 263169

I hope you have enjoyed these methods a lot. The best part of this method is that you get the answer in no time with minimal chance of error. Let's now move to some other special methods which might look tough in comparison with the method discussed above but I promise you that once you start practising it you will find it much easier to understand. A second look at the rules will help you generalize the method on your own, which will make the understanding of this method easy. So why don't you take up the challenge and solve these questions?

Find the Square of the Following:–

a) 17   b) 29   c) 38   d) 43   e) 57   f) 69
g) 121 h) 241 i) 341 j) 508 k) 985 l) 328

7

A Special Method for Square

In the previous chapter you have learnt several methods of squaring a number. I hope they have given you an extra edge over your friend in terms of speed and accuracy. But somehow you still think that you need some superfast method for squaring, isn't it? This supplementary chapter will give directions to your need and I am hopeful that you will learn some new tricks here which will prove beneficial to you.

Before I proceed, let me put a question to you:–
1) 1254 × 7658 = ?
2) 1254 × 7000 = ?

Which one of the above two multiplications can you do in your mind?

Absolutely right! The second one.

Can you figure out the reason behind it?

It is very simple to multiply any number with a number with maximum zeros. I shall use the same technique in squaring a number. One request I would like to make here is that you turn the pages back and go through the methods discussed in the multiplication chapters, chapters 3 and 4, for better understanding.

Now let me open the Pandora's box for you.

Squaring a Two-Digit Number

The modus operandi of this technique is to find two numbers from the numbers to be squared in such a way that one is the multiple of 10s. Let me put identifiers for you:

$$A^2 = (A+D)(A-D) + D^2$$

In the above identifiers A is the number to be squared and D is the number that makes one of the pairs of A in the multiple of 10. Suppose you have to find the square of 14, then obviously if you subtract 4 from it you will get 10 which has a zero. Let me illustrate the modus operandi in detail.

Example:– Find the square of 14

Solution:– As discussed in the multiplication chapter, we are trying to find out the nearest base numbers and convert the number to be squared in excess and deficit of the base. The excess and deficit is then multiplied and the square of the difference is then added to get the result.

$$14^2 = 14 \begin{smallmatrix} +4 \nearrow 18 \\ \times \\ -4 \searrow 10 \end{smallmatrix} 180 + 4 \times 4 = 196$$

Example:– Find the square of 36

Solution:– As discussed above that we have to add and subtract a number that makes one of the numbers a multiple of 10. Find the product of these two numbers and square the number added/subtracted.

$$36^2 = 36 \begin{smallmatrix} +6 \nearrow 42 \\ \times \\ -6 \searrow 30 \end{smallmatrix} 1260 + 6^2 = 1296$$

Example:– Find the square of 84

Solution:– In order to find the square we simply add and subtract 4 in 84; the two numbers thus obtained will be multiplied and the square of 4 will be further added.

$$84^2 = 84 \begin{array}{c} +4 \nearrow 88 \\ \times | \\ -4 \searrow 80 \end{array} 7040 + 4^2 = 7056$$

Example:– Find the square of 187

Solution:– Adding and subtracting 7 will make the product of two numbers difficult.

$$187^2 = 187 \begin{array}{c} +7 \nearrow 194 \\ \times | \\ -7 \searrow 180 \end{array}$$

Let's think the other combination which can make our calculation easier.

$$187^2 = 187 \begin{array}{c} +13 \nearrow 200 \\ \times | \\ -13 \searrow 174 \end{array} 34800 + 13^2$$

The square of 13 can be done in this manner.

$$13 \begin{array}{c} +3 \nearrow 16 \\ \\ -3 \searrow 10 \end{array} 160 + 3^2 = 169$$

Hence,

$$187^2 = 187 \begin{array}{c} +13 \nearrow 200 \\ \times | \\ -13 \searrow 174 \end{array} 34800 + 13^2 = 34800 + 169 = 34969$$

Example:– Find the square of 948

Solution:– Let's see the working in detail:

$$948^2 = 948 \begin{array}{c} +52 \nearrow 1000 \\ | \\ -52 \searrow 896 \end{array} 896000 + 52^2 = 896000 + 2704 = 898704$$

$$52 \begin{array}{c} +2 \nearrow 54 \\ \\ -2 \searrow 50 \end{array} 2700 + 2 \times 2 + 2704$$

Example:– Find the square of 1029
Solution:– The working is shown here:

$$1029^2 = 1029 \begin{matrix} {\scriptstyle +29} \nearrow 1058 \searrow \\ \times | \\ {\scriptstyle -29} \searrow 1000 \nearrow \end{matrix} 1058000 + 29^2 = 1058841$$

$$29 \begin{matrix} {\scriptstyle +9} \nearrow 38 \searrow \\ \\ {\scriptstyle -9} \searrow 20 \nearrow \end{matrix} 760 + 9^2 = 841$$

I do hope the above examples are enough to work as a catalyst to motivate you to take some other examples and work out independently. Initially you could make use of a calculator to check your calculation.

There are several methods in Vedic Mathematics to find the square of a number which I have discussed in my book *The Essentials of Vedic Mathematics*. These will prove handy if you want to understand the concept of Vedic Mathematics and do fast calculation. I am explaining here one of the highly recommended square methods, which I personally use and teach during my lectures in schools or elsewhere. Let's unearth its beauty.

Duplex Method of Finding Square of a Number

By using this sutra we can find the square of any number, of any length, with comfort and ease in one line. This is unique in the sense that it has universal application. Let us denote the duplex of a number by **D**.

- Duplex of 1-digit number = Square of that number
    D(a) = a^2
  Duplex of 2 = 2^2 = 4
  Duplex of 6 = 6^2 = 36

- Duplex of 2-digit number = 2 × (Product of digits)
    D(ab) = 2ab
  Duplex of 24 = 2 × (2 × 4) = 24
  Duplex of 76 = 2 × (7 × 6) = 84

- Duplex of 3-digit number = 2 × (1ˢᵗ digit × 3ʳᵈ digit) + (square of middle digit)

    $D(abc) = 2ac + b^2$

    Duplex of 126 = 2 × (1 × 6) + 2^2 = 16
    Duplex of 478 = 2 × (4 × 8) + 7^2 = 113

- Duplex of 4-digit number = 2 × (1ˢᵗ digit × 4ᵗʰ digit) + 2 × (2ⁿᵈ digit × 3ʳᵈ digit).

    $D(abcd) = 2ad + 2bc$

    Duplex of 2468 = 2 × (2 × 8) + 2 × (4 × 6) = 80
    Duplex of 4567 = 2 × (4 × 7) + 2 × (5 × 6) = 116

- Duplex of 5-digit number = 2 × (1ˢᵗ digit × 5ᵗʰ digit) + 2 × (2ⁿᵈ digit × 4ᵗʰ digit) + (middle digit)²

    $D(abcde) = 2ae + 2bd + c^2$

    Duplex of 16289 = 2 × (1 × 9) + 2 × (6 × 8) + 2^2 = 118
    Duplex of 50406 = 2 × (5 × 6) + 2 × (0 × 0) + 4^2 = 76

Example:– Find the square of 49

Solution:– The groups for **49** are

$$= \underbrace{4^2}_{D(4)} \mid \underbrace{2 \times 4 \times 9}_{D(49)} \mid \underbrace{9^2}_{D(9)}$$

= 16 | 7 2 | 8 1

= 16 / 80 / 1
= 2401

Example:– Find the square of 465

Solution:– The groups of numbers for **465** are-

$$= \underbrace{4^2}_{D(4)} \quad \underbrace{2 \times 4 \times 6}_{D(46)} \quad \underbrace{2 \times 4 \times 5 + 6^2}_{D(465)} \quad \underbrace{2 \times 6 \times 5}_{D(65)} \quad \underbrace{5^2}_{D(5)}$$

= 16 | 48 | 76 | 60 | 25

= 20 / ₁5/₁ 2/2/5
= 216225

Example:– Find the square of 8254

Solution:– The groups of numbers for 8254 are
8, 82, 825, 8254, 254, 54 and 4.

Duplex of $8 = 8^2 = 64$
Duplex of $82 = 2 \times 8 \times 2 = 32$
Duplex of $825 = 2 \times 8 \times 5 + 2^2 = 84$
Duplex of $8254 = 2 \times 8 \times 4 + 2 \times 2 \times 5 = 84$
Duplex of $254 = 2 \times 2 \times 4 + 3^2 = 41$
Duplex of $54 = 2 \times 5 \times 4 = 40$
Duplex of $4 = 4^2 = 16$

Arrange the values of duplex as follows-
64 | $_3$2 | $_8$4 | $_8$4 | $_4$1 | $_4$0 | $_1$6
= 6 8 1 2 8 5 1 6
Hence $(8254)^2 = 68128516$

After a little practice you will master this method and be able to do the squaring of a number of any length on your own. Now I am leaving you with this Vedic method to practise some examples.

Find the square of the following by Duplex Method

a) 65   b) 74   c) 89   d) 91
e) 456   f) 674   g) 896   h) 997
i) 1234 j) 2126 k) 4214 l) 9862

In order to make the squaring more interesting I am now going to add the squaring method of numbers that end with 1, 2, 3, etc. Let's practise and get a command over it.

a) **When the unit digit is** 1:– Follow the following steps
   i) Subtract 1 from the number and square the result
   ii) Add twice the subtracted number in previous result
   iii) Add 1

Example:– Find the square of 21

Solution:– i) Subtract 1 = 21 − 1 = 20

ii) Square the previous result = 20^2 = 400
iii) Add twice the result of step 1 into step 2 = 400 + 2 × 20 = 440
iv) Add 1 to the previous result = 440 + 1 = 441

Hence, $(21)^2 = 441$

Example:— Find the square of 91

Solution:— i) Subtract 1 = 91 − 1 = 90
ii) Square the previous result = 90^2 = 8100
iii) Add twice the result of step 1 into step 2 = 8100 + 2 × 90 = 8280
iv) Add 1 to the previous result = 8280 + 1 = 8281

Hence, $(91)^2 = 8281$

b) **When the unit digit is 2:—** Follow the given steps

i) Since the unit digit of the number to be squared is 2 the unit digit of square should be 4
ii) Multiply the ten's digit by 4
iii) Find the square of ten's digit
iv) Keep all the digits in a digit separator and in case there are two digits in any of the separator line, move the extreme digit into the next separator.

The whole process can be written in a single line:

$$(A2)^2 = A^2 / 4A / 4$$

Example:— Find the square of 32

Solution:— i) Unit digit = 4
ii) Multiply the ten's digit by 4 = 3 × 4 = 12
iii) Find the square of ten's digit = 3^2 = 9
iv) Keep all the digits in a separator as shown below

9 / 12 / 4
= 1024

The extreme 1 of second separator is moved into the third column and added.

Example:– Find the square of 62

Solution:–
i) Unit digit = 4
ii) Multiply the ten's digit by 4 = 6 × 4 = 24
iii) Find the square of ten's digit = 6^2 = 6
iv) Keep all the digits in a separator as shown here–

$$36 \, / \, 24 \, / \, 4$$
$$= 3844$$

Example:– Find the square of 42

Solution:– $(42)^2 = 4^2 \, / \, 4 \times 4 \, / \, 4$
$= 16 \, / \, 16 \, / \, 4$
$= 1764$

Example:– Find the square of 82

Solution:– $(82)^2 = 8^2 \, / \, 4 \times 8 \, / \, 4$
$= 64 \, / \, 32 \, / \, 4$
$= 6724$

c) **When the unit digit is 3:–** The whole process can be understood in a single line

$$(A3)^2 = A^2 \, / \, 6A \, / \, 9$$

Let me take some examples to make the whole process easier.

Example:– Find the square of 43

Solution:–
i) Unit digit = 9
ii) Multiply the ten's digit by 6 = 6 × 4 = 24
iii) Find the square of ten's digit = 4^2 = 16
iv) Keep all the digits in a separator as shown below

$$16 \, / \, 24 \, / \, 9$$
$$= 1849$$

Example:- Find the square of 93

Solution:-
i) Unit digit = 9
ii) Multiply the ten's digit by 6 = 6 × 9 = 54
iii) Find the square of ten's digit = 9^2 = 81
iv) Keep all the digits in a separator as shown below

81 /54 / 9
= 8649

Example:- Find the square of 73?

Solution:- $(73)^2 = 7^2$ / 7 × 6 / 9
= 49 / 42 / 9
= 5329

Example:- Find the square of 53?

Solution:- $(53)^2 = 5^2$ / 5 × 6 / 9
= 25 / 30 / 9
= 2809

d) **When the unit digit is 4:–** As discussed in the method earlier the square of a digit ending with 4 will have 6 at its unit digit. Without wasting time in details, let's do the whole process in a single line.

$$(A4)^2 = A^2 / 8A + 1 / 6$$

Example:- Find the square of 74?

Solution:-
a) The digit at ten's place = 7 = A (say). Square it and you get 7^2 = 49
b) 8 × ten's digit + 1 = 8 × 7 + 1 = 57
c) Place 6 at the unit digit.

$(74)^2$ = 49 / 57 / 6
= 49 + 5/ 7 / 6 = 5476

Example:– Find the square of 94

Solution:– a) The digit at ten's place = 9 = A (say). Square it and you get $9^2 = 81$
b) 8 × ten's digit + 1 = 8 × 9 + 1 = 73
c) Place 6 at the unit digit.

$$(94)^2 = 81 / 73 / 6$$
$$= 81 + 7/ 3 / 6 = 8836$$

Example:– Find the square of 44

Solution:– $(44)^2 = 4^2 / 8 \times 4 + 1/ 6$

$$= 16 / 33 / 6$$
$$= 1936$$

Example:– Find the square of 64

Solution:– $(64)^2 = 6^2 / 8 \times 6 + 1/ 6$

$$= 36 / 49 / 6$$
$$= 4096$$

e) **When the unit digit is 5:–** Squaring a number ending with 5 is so simple that even a Grade 2 child can do it if directed correctly. The modus operandi is also very simple.

$$(A5)^2 = A \times (A + 1) / 25$$

Example:– Find the square of 75

Solution:– $(75)^2 = 7 \times 8 / 25$
$$= 5625$$

Example:– Find the square of 95

Solution:– $(95)^2 = 9 \times 10 / 25$
$$= 9025$$

Example:– Find the square of 65

Solution:– $(65)^2 = 6 \times 7 / 25$
$= 4225$

Example:– Find the square of 105

Solution:– $(105)^2 = 10 \times 11 / 25$
$= 11025$

f) **When the unit digit is 6:**– Squaring a number ending with 6 will have three parts. It involves the following steps:–

   a) Unit digit of square will be 6
   b) The second part of the operation will be: 2 × ten's digit + 3
   c) Ten's digit × next digit

The whole operation can be summed up in one line.

$(A6)^2 = A \times (A+1) / 2A + 3 / 6$

Example:– Find the square of 56

Solution:– $(56)^2$ = Ten's digit × next digit / 2 × ten's digit + 3 / 6
$= 5 \times 6 / 2 \times 5 + 3 / 6$
$= 30 / 13 / 6$
$= 3136$

Example:– Find the square of 96

Solution:– $(96)^2 = 9 \times 10 / 2 \times 9 + 3 / 6$
$= 90 / 21 / 6$
$= 9216$

Example:– Find the square of 76

Solution:– $(76)^2 = 7 \times 8 / 2 \times 7 + 3 / 6$
$= 56 / 17 / 6$
$= 5776$

Example:– Find the square of 46

Solution:– $(46)^2 = 4 \times 5 / 2 \times 4 + 3 / 6$
$\qquad\quad\ = 20/ 11 / 6$
$\qquad\quad\ = 2116$

g) **When the unit digit is 7:–** Squaring a number ending with 7 will have the following steps:–

   a) Unit digit of square will be 9
   b) The second part of the operation will be: 4 × ten's digit + 4
   c) Ten's digit × Next digit

The whole operation can be summed up in one line.

$(A7)^2 = A \times (A+1) / 4A + 4 /9$

Example:– Find the square of 77

Solution:– $(77)^2 = 7 \times 8 / 4 \times 7 + 4 /9$
$\qquad\quad\ = 56/ 32 / 9$
$\qquad\quad\ = 5929$

Example:– Find the square of 37

Solution:– $(37)^2 = 3 \times 4 / 4 \times 3 + 4 /9$
$\qquad\quad\ = 12/ 16 /9$
$\qquad\quad\ = 1369$

Example:– Find the square of 67

Solution:– $(67)^2 = 6 \times 7 / 6 \times 4 + 4 /9$
$\qquad\quad\ = 42/ 28 /9$
$\qquad\quad\ = 4489$

Example:– Find the square of 97

Solution:– $(97)^2 = 9 \times 10 / 4 \times 9 + 4 /9$
$\qquad\quad\ = 90/ 40 /9$
$\qquad\quad\ = 9409$

h) **When the unit digit is 8:–** Squaring a number ending with 8 will have the following steps:–

   a) Unit digit of square will be 4
   b) The second part of the operation will be: 6 × ten's digit + 6
   c) Ten's digit × Next digit

The whole operation can be summed up in one line.

$(A8)^2 = A \times (A+1) / 6A + 6 / 4$

Example:– Find the square of 48

Solution:– $(48)^2 = 4 \times 5 / 6 \times 4 + 6 / 4$
$= 20 / 30 / 4$
$= 2304$

Example:– Find the square of 68

Solution:– $(68)^2 = 6 \times 7 / 6 \times 6 + 6 / 4$
$= 42 / 42 / 4$
$= 4624$

Example:– Find the square of 88

Solution:– $(88)^2 = 8 \times 9 / 6 \times 8 + 6 / 4$
$= 72 / 54 / 4$
$= 7744$

Example:– Find the square of 98

Solution:– $(98)^2 = 9 \times 10 / 6 \times 9 + 6 / 4$
$= 90 / 60 / 4$
$= 9604$

Example:– Find the square of 28

Solution:– $(28)^2 = 2 \times 3 / 6 \times 2 + 6 / 4$
$= 6 / 18 / 4$
$= 784$

i) **When the unit digit is 9:–** Squaring a number ending with 8 will have the following steps:–
   a) Unit digit of square will be 1
   b) The second part of the operation will be: 8 × ten's digit + 8
   c) Ten's digit × Next digit

The whole operation can be summed up in one line.

$(A9)^2 = A \times (A+1) / 8A + 8 / 1$

Example:– Find the square of 49

Solution:– $(49)^2 = 4 \times 5 / 8 \times 4 + 8 / 1$
$= 20 / 40 / 1$
$= 2401$

Example:– Find the square of 69

Solution:– $(69)^2 = 6 \times 7 / 8 \times 6 + 8 / 1$
$= 42 / 54 / 1$
$= 4741$

Example:– Find the square of 89

Solution:– $(89)^2 = 8 \times 9 / 8 \times 8 + 8 / 1$
$= 72 / 72 / 1$
$= 7921$

Example:– Find the square of 99

Solution:– $(99)^2 = 9 \times 10 / 8 \times 9 + 8 / 1$
$= 90 / 80 / 1$
$= 9801$

Example:– Find the square of 29

Solution:– $(29)^2 = 2 \times 3 / 8 \times 2 + 8 / 1$
$= 6 / 24 / 1$
$= 841$

I think I have opened up everything in front of you that I had taught so far in the two chapters on squaring, with ample examples discussed to make you a maths wizard. So let's do some practice to strengthen your skills.

a) 89
b) 67
c) 92
d) 765
e) 41
f) 72
g) 83
h) 64
i) 75
j) 86
k) 97
l) 88

8

Square Root Is Not Tough

If you square 2, you get 4, and if you 'take the square root of 4', you get 2; if you square 3, you get 9, and if you 'take the square root of 9', you get 3.

Mathematically, if $x^2 = y$ then $x = y^{1/2} = \pm \sqrt{y}$

$2^2 = 4$, so $\sqrt{4} = 2$
$3^2 = 9$, so $\sqrt{9} = 3$

Square root of a perfect square number is generally extracted by two methods:–

a) Prime factorization method
b) Division method

But both the methods have their drawbacks. In this chapter, I shall explore the guessing technique which works better as far as the extraction of perfect square root is concerned.

Before I begin with the new method let us understand the following fundamental rules.

- A perfect square ends in 0, 1, 4, 5, 6 and 9.
- A number is not a perfect square if it ends with 2, 3, 7 or 8.
- If the given number has n digits then its square root will have n/2 digits if n is even else (n + 1)/ 2 digits if n is odd.

Let us study the following square root table.

Table 8.1

N	N^2	Last digit of N^2	Digit sum of number
1	1	1	1
2	4	4	4
3	9	9	9
4	16	6	7
5	25	5	7
6	36	6	9
7	49	9	4
8	64	4	1
9	81	1	9
10	100	00	1

From the above table we conclude that:

1. A complete square ending in 1 must have either 1 or 9 as the last digit of square root.
2. A square ending in 4 must have 2 or 8 as the last digit of square root.
3. A square ending in 6 must have 4 or 6 as the last digit of square root.
4. A square ending in 5 will have 5 as the last digit of the square root.
5. A square ending in 9 must have 3 or 7 as the last digit of square root.
6. A square ending in 00 will have 0 as the last digit of square root.

Apart from the above observations, let us look at the following Nearest Square Root table that will help us to find the square root of a number instantly.

Square Root Is Not Tough 111

Table 8.2

Number	Nearest Square Root	Number	Nearest Square Root
1-3	1	4-8	2
9-15	3	16-24	4
25-35	5	36-48	6
49-63	7	64-80	8

The above two tables will help you calculate the square root of any 3- or 4-digit number whose square root comes in 2 digits. But before I proceed to the mental exercises let me warm you up with some unique methods.

Extracting Square Root Using $(a + b)^2 = a^2 + 2ab + b^2$

Most of you would remember the formula:– $(a + b)^2 = a^2 + 2ab + b^2$. Now I shall use this formula to extract the square root of any 3- or 4-digit number. The modus operandi is explained here, which will be discussed once again in the examples.

Rule:–

1. First place the dot, from right to left in pairs of two, placing dots or bar above the numbers in group.
2. Find the first digit of the square root from the above table. Say it is **a**.
3. Subtract a^2 from the first pair and bring the next digit of dividend down as done in ordinary division.
4. Your next mission is to find **b** as shown in the expansion using **2ab** and placing the value of **a** extracted in the first step. Equate the result obtained in step 3 to **2ab** such that the value of **b** placed in **2ab** gives you less than or equal to the value of the result obtained in step 3.
5. The best part of this method is that you can counter-check your calculation by comparing b^2 with the final remainder.

Let us take some examples to understand the method in a better fashion.

Example:– Find the square root of 225.

Solution:– First place the dot making a group of 2 from right to left. The number of groups will decide the number of digits in the given square root. Here we have two groups so the answer will have exactly 2 digits. See its detailed working with illustrations.

$$1 \begin{array}{|cc|} \overline{2} & \overline{25} \\ -1 & \downarrow \\ \hline 1 & 2 \\ -1 & 0 \\ \hline & 25 \end{array} \begin{array}{l} a = 1 \\ b = 5 \end{array}$$

Here, $a = 1$ because $1^2 \leq 2 \leq 2^2$. Now we subtract $a^2 = 1$ from 2 and carry down the next digit of dividend. Now our aim is to find the value of b so as to complete the square root process.

i.e. $2 \times 1 \times b \leq 12$

Hence, $b \leq 6$

If you take $b = 6$ then $12 - 2ab = 0$. This will make $b^2 = 36$ but now you are only left with a single digit 5 at the end. So you have to take $b = 5$.

For $b = 5$, $12 - 2ab = 12 - 2 \times 1 \times 5 = 2$

Carry down the next digit 5 which will make your next remainder 25 which is equal to b^2

Example:– Find the square root of 8836.

Solution:– Group the digits in pairs and do as described.

$$9 \begin{array}{|cc|} \overline{36} & \overline{36} \\ -81 & \\ \hline 73 & \\ -72 & \\ \hline & 16 \end{array} \begin{array}{l} a = 9 \\ b = 4 \end{array}$$

$9^2 \leq 88 \leq 10^2$

Hence a = 9

Subtract a^2 from the first group and bring the immediate next digit of dividend down.

88 − 81 = 7. After bringing the next digit 3 our next new dividend = 73

Take a value of b such that 2ab ≤73

2 × 9 × b ≤ 73.

Hence, b = 4 because for b = 5 we get 90 which is greater than 73

Subtract 73 − 2ab = 73 − 72 = 1

Carry down the next digit from the dividend which makes our new dividend = 16

Once you find the value of b you can check whether b^2 = remaining pair of dividend.

Hence, a = 9 and b = 4

Interesting and Superb Method to Extract Square Root Mentally

Let me explain one very interesting method of extracting the square root of any 3- or 4-digit number effortlessly.

Rule:−

- Ignore the last two digits of the group and find the value of **a** from Table 8.1.
- Obtain the last two digits of the square root from Table 8.2. If the last digit of the square root to be extracted is 1, 4, 6, 9 then you will have two possibilities of answer which will be determined in the next step.
- Multiply **a by a + 1**. If the product **a × (a + 1) > first part of the group** then the smaller of the two possible numbers will be taken.
- In case **a × (a + 1) ≤ first part of the group**; take the higher possible value for **b**.

Example:− Find the square root of 2304

Solution:– First, group the number in pairs.

$$\overline{23}\ \overline{04}$$

Ignore the last pair and find the value of **a** from the given Table 8.2.

$$4^2 < 23 < 5^2$$

Here, a = 4

Since the last digit of the number is 4 we will have two possible answers for **b**. It is either 2 or 8.

Multiply a = 4 by a + 1 = 5
$$4 \times 5 = 20 < 23 \text{ (first pair of group)}$$
Hence b = 8 (larger of two possible values)
$$\sqrt{2304} = 48$$

Example:– Find the square root of 676

Solution:– We have two groups here. 6 and 76. Ignore the last group 76 and find the value of **a** for the first group.

$$2^2 < 6 < 3^2$$
Hence, a = 2

As you can see the last digit of 676 is 6 so from Table 8.1, we get two possible sets of answers for **b**, i.e. 4 and 6.

Multiply a = 2 by a + 1 = 3
$$2 \times 3 = 6 = 6 \text{ (first pair of group)}$$
Hence b = 6 (larger of two possible values)
Therefore, $\sqrt{676} = 26$

Example:– Find the square root of 8836

Solution:– We have two groups here—88 and 36. Ignore the last group 36 and find the value of **a** for the first group.
$$9^2 < 88 < 10^2$$
Hence, a = 9

As you can see the last digit of 8836 is 6 so from Table 8.1, we get two possible sets of answer for b, i.e. 4 and 6.

Multiply a = 9 by a + 1 = 10

$$9 \times 10 = 90 > 88 \text{ (first pair of group)}$$

Hence b = 4 (smaller of two possible values)

Therefore, $\sqrt{8836} = 94$

Square Root of 5-6 Digits

Rule:-

- Make a group of two digits starting from the right. Here we will have three groups. Denote the left digit by L, the middle digit by M and the right digit by R.
- The first (L) and third (R) group will give us the hundred's place digit and the unit place digit. These two can be written through observation, with the help of Table 8.1 and Table 8.2.
- Subtract L^2 from the first pair and carry down the next digit from the dividend, as done in simple division.
- Compare the new dividend by 2 L M. Put different value of M in 2 L M and select the best possible digit, so that 2 L M ≤ new dividend.
- In order to avoid confusion over the choice of the number, use the Casting out Nines rule.
- Exact square root = L M R

Example 1:- Find the square root of 692224.

Solution:-

- Make a group of two digits, starting from the right.

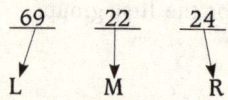

- Since the unit digit of the given number ends with 4, therefore the square root ends in 2 or 8 (Table 8.1).
- 69 in the left group lies between $8^2 < 64 < 9^2$, hence, L = 8 (Table 8.2).
- Now subtract L^2 from the given number and carry down the next digit from the dividend as shown below

$$\begin{array}{ccc} 69 & 22 & 24 \\ -8^2 & & \\ \hline 5 & 2 & \end{array}$$

→ carry down the next digit from the dividend
→ new dividend

- Compare the new dividend by 2 L M = 2 × 8 × M = 16 M. Put different values of M.
  For M = 3, 16 × 3 = 48 < 52
  and For M = 4, 64 > 52. Hence, M = 3
- Now we are left with two options:–
  $\sqrt{69\ 22\ 24}$ = 8 3 2 or 8 3 8
- Apply the Casting out Nines method to overcome the confusion in selecting the correct answer.

Digit sum of 69 22 24	Digit sum of $(832)^2$	Digit sum of $(838)^2$
6 + 9 + 2 + 2 + 2 + 4 = 7	7	1

Hence, $\sqrt{69\ 22\ 24}$ = 832

Example 1:– Find the square root of 218089

Solution:–
- Make a group of two digits, starting from the right.

$$\underset{L}{21} \quad \underset{M}{80} \quad \underset{R}{89}$$

- Since the unit digit of the given number ends with 9, the square root ends in 3 or 7 (Table 8.1)

Square Root Is Not Tough

- 21 in the left group lies between $4^2 < 21 < 5^2$, hence, L = 4 (Table 8.2)
- Now subtract L^2 from the given number and carry down the next digit from the dividend as shown below

```
  21    80    89
 - 4²    ↓
  ───────────────→ carry down the next digit from the dividend
   5    8 ──────→ new dividend
```

- Compare the new dividend by 2 L M = 2 × 4 × M = 8 M. Put different values of M.
  For M = 6, 8 × 6 = 48 < 58
  and For M = 7, 56 < 58. Hence, M = 6 or 7
- Now we are left with four options:–
  $\sqrt{21\ 80\ 89}$ = 463, 467, 473 or 479
- Apply the Casting out Nines method to overcome the confusion in selecting the correct answer.

Digit sum of 218089	Digit sum of $(463)^2$	Digit sum of $(467)^2$	Digit sum of $(473)^2$	Digit sum of $(479)^2$
1	7	1	5	4

This clearly shows
$\sqrt{2\ 1\ 8\ 0\ 8\ 9}$ = 467

The estimation for more than two options can be established by the Casting out Nines method. The details of this method can be found in my book *The Essentials of Vedic Mathematics*. With a little practice you can find the square root of a perfect square in seconds. So take the challenge and do these questions to improve your calculating ability.

Find the square root of the following:–

a) 232324 b) 126736 c) 3969 d) 2401
e) 7921   f) 4624   g) 9604 h) 4761

In order to calculate the square root mentally, you have to practise, practise and practise and in a week or two you will gain mastery over finding the square root of any number which is a perfect square.

Before I wind up this chapter let me discuss a method to find the square root of irrational numbers and that too just by estimation. Irrational numbers are numbers whose perfect square root cannot be estimated and you will have to make use of the Division Method only as the Factor Method will not come in handy in such a situation. You will find this method handy especially in trigonometry and mensuration.

Square root of irrational number =

$$\sqrt{\text{Nearest perfect square}} + \frac{\text{Deviation from irrational number}}{2 \times \sqrt{\text{Nearest perfect square}}}$$

Let us see a few examples to understand the modus operandi of extracting the square root of a number that is not a perfect square.

Example:– Find the square root of 47

Solution:– Perfect square approaching 47 is 49.

Deviation = 47 − 49 = − 2

$\sqrt{47} = \sqrt{49} - \dfrac{2}{2 \times \sqrt{49}}$

$= 7 - 1/7 = 7 - 0.14 = 6.86$

Example:– Find the square root of 174

Solution:– Perfect square approaching 174 is 169

Deviation = 174 − 169 = 5

$\sqrt{174} = \sqrt{169} + \dfrac{5}{2 \times \sqrt{169}}$

$= 13 + 5/26$

$= 13.192$

I hope you have enjoyed your journey with square roots and that you get mastery over it with practice in due course of time.

9

Cube: A Piece of Cake

Cube of a number is multiplication of that number by itself three times.

For example, if you are asked to find the cube of 2, you will multiply 2 by 2 three times. In the same fashion the cube of a number 3 is $3 \times 3 \times 3$.

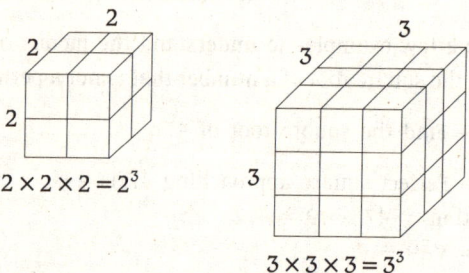

$2 \times 2 \times 2 = 2^3$

$3 \times 3 \times 3 = 3^3$

The conventional method of cubing a number is time-consuming as far as numbers of 2 or 3 digits are concerned. But the method discussed here is simple and perfect and you can calculate in an easy manner provided you have learnt the cube of first ten numbers.

Let me put down a table for you to memorize before I start the shortcut method of calculation.

Table 9.1

Number	1	2	3	4	5	6	7	8	9	10
Cube	1	8	27	64	125	216	343	512	729	1000

Table 9.1 will help you to calculate fast. Let me start with a simple method of cubing a number. Before I start I shall advise you to go to the multiplication chapters once again and revise the method of multiplying two consecutive numbers, etc.

Here is the method for your convenience.

$$\begin{aligned} a^3 &= a^3 - a + a \\ &= a(a^2 - 1) + a \\ &= a(a + 1)(a - 1) + a \\ &= (a - 1) \times a \times (a + 1) + a \end{aligned}$$

What I want you to see through this detailed expansion of the formula is that you are going to multiply three consecutive numbers. In the chapter on multiplication in this book I have given a detailed method of multiplying consecutive numbers.

Example:– Find the cube of 11

Solution:– Here a = 11, so the preceding and succeeding numbers for 11 are 10 and 12. Multiply these three numbers and add 11 to get the result. The diagram below will help you understand the method.

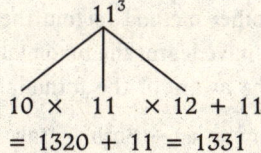

= 1320 + 11 = 1331

Example:– Find the cube of 25

Solution:– Here a = 25 and its preceding and succeeding numbers are 24 and 26. Let's see how it works. Here the shortcut method of multiplying any number by 25 will be helpful.

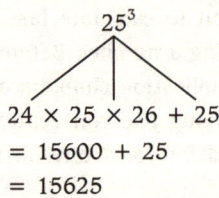

$$= 15600 + 25$$
$$= 15625$$

Example:– Find the cube of 99

Solution:– For a = 99, the preceding and succeeding numbers are 98 and 100. You know how easy it is to multiply a number by 100 so what are you waiting for? Let's do the calculation:

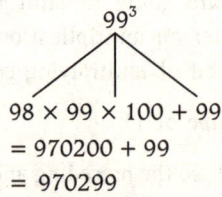

$$= 970200 + 99$$
$$= 970299$$

Multiplication of any number by 99 is easy and if you have gone through the chapters suggested you will not have any problem in multiplying these three numbers.

Let's use some other method to find the cube of a number.

Most of you who have learnt the binomial expansion in upper primary level must be aware of the formula:

$$(a + b)^3 = a^3 + 3a^2b + 3ab^2 + b^3$$

Let's do some manipulation to the formula and simplify it according to our needs.

$a^3 = a^2 \times a \qquad 3a^2b = a^2 \times 3b \qquad 3ab^2 = b^2 \times 3a \qquad b^3 = b \times b^2$

Example:– Find the cube of 23

Solution:– Here, a = 2 and b = 3
$$a^3 = a^2 \times a = 2^2 \times 2 = 8$$
$$a^2 \times 3b = 2^2 \times 3 \times 3 = 36$$

$$b^2 \times 3a = 3^2 \times 3 \times 2 = 54$$
$$b^3 = b^2 \times b = 3^2 \times 3 = 27$$

Arrange these numbers as shown here and keep only one number in each part, moving the rest to the previous part.

$$(23)^3 = 8 / 36 / 54 / 27$$
$$= 8 + 3 + 1/1/6/7$$
$$= 12167$$

Example:– Find the cube of 35

Solution:– Here, a = 3 and b = 5
$$a^3 = a^2 \times a = 3^2 \times 3 = 27$$
$$a^2 \times 3b = 3^2 \times 3 \times 5 = 135$$
$$b^2 \times 3a = 5^2 \times 3 \times 3 = 225$$
$$b^3 = b^2 \times b = 5^2 \times 5 = 125$$

Arrange these numbers as shown here and keep only one number in each part, moving the rest to the previous part.

$$(35)^3 = 27 / 135 / 225 / 125$$
$$= 27 / 135 / 225 + 12 = 237 / 5$$
$$= 27 / 135 + 23 = 158 / 7 / 5$$
$$= 27 + 15 / 8 / 7 / 5$$
$$= 42875$$

Let's simplify the process a little.

Cube of a Number Near Base

The method we are discussing here will make the cubing process a little better and you will enjoy doing it. I think I need not focus on the word base here as we have spent ample time doing so in the multiplication part. Base numbers are the multiples of 10. First loot at the rule of cubing for a number near its base.

Deviation = Difference of a number from its base. If the

number to be cubed is closer to the base number 10^n (10, 100, 1000...) then you don't need any sub-base. On the other hand if your base number is 20, 30, 40, 50... then sub-base = multiples of base number in the form of 10^n.

- The whole cubing process involves 3 steps.
  A) (Number to be cubed + 2 × deviation from the base) × (sub-base)^2
  B) {3 × (deviation)^2} × sub-base
  C) (Deviation)^3
- If there is no sub-base, then the calculation becomes very easy.

Example:– Find the cube of 15

Solution:– 15 is nearer to the base 10.
Deviation = 15 − 10 = 5
$(15)^3 = \underbrace{15 + 2 \times 5}_{1^{st} \text{ term}} \mid \underbrace{3 \times (5)^2}_{2^{nd} \text{ term}} \mid \underbrace{(5)^3}_{3^{rd} \text{ term}}$
= 2 5 | 7 5 | 12 5
= 3375

Example:– Find the cube of 98

Solution:– 98 is nearer to the base 100.
Deviation = 98 − 100 = −2
Hence $(98)^3 = \underbrace{98 + 2 \times (-2)}_{1^{st} \text{ term}} \mid \underbrace{3 \times (-2)^2}_{2^{nd} \text{ term}} \mid \underbrace{(-2)^3}_{3^{rd} \text{ term}}$
= 94 | 12 | −8
= 94 | 11 | 100 − 8
= 94 | 11 | 92
Hence $(98)^3 = 941192$

Example:– Find the cube of 106

Solution:– Working base = 100
Deviation = 106 − 100 = 6

$$(106)^3 = 106 + 6 \times 2 \mid 3 \times 6^2 \mid 6^3$$
$$= 118 \mid 108 \mid 216$$
$$= 1191016$$

(Since the base = 100, there should be 2 digits in each digit separator)

Example:– Find the cube of 26

Solution:– Since 26 is far from the working base 10, we will have to take 20 as a working base.

For $26 = 2 \times 10 + 6$
Base = 10 Sub-base = 2 Deviation = 6
$$(26)^3 = 2^2 \times \{26 + 2 \times 6\} \mid 2 \times 3 \times 6^2 \mid 6^3$$
$$= 152 \mid 21\ 6 \mid 21\ 6$$
$$= 17576$$

Example:– Find the cube of 208

Solution:– $208 = 2 \times 100 + 8$
  Base = 100   Sub-Base = 2   Deviation = 8
$$(208)^3 = (208 + 2 \times 8) \times 2^2 \mid 2 \times 3 \times 8^2 \mid 8^3$$
$$= 896 \mid 384 \mid 5\ 12$$
$$= 8998912$$

Once again, on the same note that only practice can make you perfect, I am winding up this chapter with the hope that you have understood the concept of cubing and you will apply the rule according to your own needs, and choose the best method you like and are comfortable with. So don't you want to try out some problems?

a) 76   b) 107   c) 206   d) 509
e) 92   f) 22   g) 72   h) 59
i) 308   j) 44   k) 379

10

Cube Root in a Playful Manner

Cube root of a number which is a perfect cube can be calculated by unconventional methods in no time. If you want to extract by the conventional method you are left with only a single option and that is the factorizing method.

Example:– Find the cube root of 592704

Solution:–

2	592704
2	296352
2	148176
2	74088
2	37044
2	18522
3	9261
3	3087
3	1029
7	343
7	49
7	7
	1

Hence, $(592704)^{1/3} = \underbrace{2 \times 2 \times 2} \times \underbrace{2 \times 2 \times 2} \times \underbrace{3 \times 3 \times 3} \times \underbrace{7 \times 7 \times 7}$
$= 2 \times 2 \times 3 \times 7$
$= 84$

The cube of a number is that number raised to the power 3 whereas the cube root of a number is 1/3 power of a number. Unlike square root, the cube root of a number has only one answer. The cube root will either be positive or negative.

Suppose $a^3 = x$
$\Rightarrow a = x^{1/3}$

The Cube Root Symbol

$\sqrt[3]{}$ is the special symbol that means 'cube root'. It is the **'radical'** symbol (used for square roots) with a small three to mean **cube root**.

You can also find the cube root of a number that is negative.

$$\sqrt[3]{-125} = -5$$

This is also due to the reason that $(-5) \times (-5) \times (-5) = -125$

Now before I start presenting the chapter I shall request you to memorize the following concept which will help you find the cube root of any number, however big it may be, instantly in 99% of the cases.

Important Points to Remember

Before we move further, look at the following table carefully. This table will help you to determine the unit digit of a cube root.

Table 10.1

If a cube ends in	The unit digit of a cube root will be
0	0
1	1
2	8
3	7

4	4
5	5
6	6
7	3
8	2
9	9

From the above table, we can conclude the following facts:–

1, 4, 5, 6, 9, and 0 repeat themselves in the cube ending.

2, 3, 7 and 8 have an interplay of complements from 10.

The left digit of a cube root having more than 7 digits, or the ten's digit of a cube root having less than 7 digits, can be extracted with the help of the following table.

Table 10.2

Left-most pair of the cube root	Nearest cube root
1 – 7	1
8 – 26	2
27 – 63	3
64 – 124	4
125 – 215	5
216 – 342	6
343 – 511	7
512 – 728	8
729 – 999	9

The above two tables will help you find the cube root of any number that has maximum 6 digits. In case there are more than 6 digits in a number, say you are going to find the cube root of a number that has 7, 8, 9 or 10 digits, you can still take the help of this table to find the **Left** and **Right** digits of that number.

- A number with maximum 6 digits will have 2 digits in its cube root.
- A number with 7-9 digits will have 3 digits in its cube root.
- The number of digits in a cube root is the same as the number of 3-digit groups in the original cube including a single digit or a double-digit group if there exists any.

I would like to mention here an important thing which will help you find the middle digits of the cube root of a number. In Vedic mathematics we discuss the **beejank** method which is similar to the Casting out Nines method or Chinese remainder theorem—to find the middle digit of the cube root. The main drawback of the Casting out Nines method is that you will have to work on several possibilities before reaching the answer but the method I shall discuss here will give you the direct answer of the middle digit. This method is called Casting out Elevens method.

Casting out Elevens

Casting out Elevens method is a method like Casting out Nines to verify the correctness of mathematical operations like ($+$, $-$, $\times$, $\div$). For detailed information on Casting out Nines; you can refer to my book *The Essentials of Vedic Mathematics*.

Do you remember the rule of checking the divisibility of any number by 11? If not, please go through the divisibility rule mentioned in Chapter 5, the division chapter. In Casting out Elevens we start with the unit digit in the one's place, then subtract the digit in ten's place, add the digit in the hundred's place, subtract the digit in the thousand's place, and continue following the same trend of alteration of addition and subtraction until we run out of digits.

Example:–

4567 in casting out nines will look like $= 7 - 6 + 5 - 4 = 12 - 10 = 2$

6790528 in casting out nines will look like $= 8 - 2 + 5 - 0 + 9 - 7 + 6 = 28 - 9 = 19 = 9 - 1 = 8$

In case the final result comes out to be a number that is greater than 10 as in the case of second example we will have to repeat the process or subtract 11 from that number. In the second example the result was $19 > 10$ so $19 - 11 = 8$ or $9 - 1 = 8$ will be written as the final sum. Always remember one thing: as in Casting out Nines, the final sum should be less than 9, in the same fashion here in Casting out Elevens the final sum should be less than 11. In other words the resultant digit should be up to 10.

Now I am going to put one more table which will help you to find the middle digit of the cube root in case the number whose cube root you want to find is more than 6 digits. The interesting part is that you can make this table on your own and find the final sum given in the table.

$(11)^3 = 1331$ and casting out eleven value is $1 - 3 + 3 - 1 = 0$
$(9)^3 = 729$ and casting out eleven value $= 9 - 2 + 7 = 14 > 11$; hence $14 - 11 = 3$.

I would advise you to formulate the table once for yourself and then see the magic. If you could remember this table like two previous tables than you will be able to find the cube root of any number up to 9 digits in seconds.

Table 10.3

N	N^3	Value in Casting out 11s	Value in Casting out 9s
0	0	0	0
1	1	1	1
2	8	8	8
3	27	5	0
4	64	9	1

5	125	4	8
6	216	7	0
7	343	2	1
8	512	6	8
9	729	3	0
10	1000	10	1

I have highlighted the value of Casting out Elevens to compare how effective the Casting out Elevens method is in finding the middle digit of cube root. If you compare the values of Casting out Nines and Casting out Elevens you will find that in Casting out Nines three values—0, 1 and 8—keep repeating. This creates a problem as you have to work out different possibilities to reach the final answer but if you see the values of Casting out Elevens you will be surprised to see that you get different values for each number. That is the best part of this method that confusion takes a back seat and that's why I prefer this method. In my previous book I had discussed the Casting out Nines method to reach the final answer of a cube root in case the number has more than 6 digits but I got hundreds of mails from my readers saying that this method to counter check is very lengthy. So, I decided to introduce something new this time and when I found that Casting out Elevens works better in this case I decided to share this method with you. It is appropriate this time as this book deals completely with shortcut methods and has nothing to do with Vedic techniques.

Let's do something new this time. Follow these examples.

Rule:–
- Form the group of three digits number from right to left. The number of groups will give you an idea of the number of digits in its cube root.
- Numbers having 4, 5 or 6 digits will have a cube root of 2 digits.

- Numbers having 7, 8 or 9 digits will have a cube root of 3 digits.
- Numbers having 10, 11 or 12 digits will have a cube root of 4 digits.

Cube Root of a Number Having 4, 5 or 6 Digits

- As mentioned above that the cube root of such numbers will have only two pairs and the unit digit of the number will decide the unit digit of the cube root, say it is R. You can decide the value of R from Table 10.1.
- If you are left with only one pair then Table 10.2 will help you to decide the ten's digit of cube root, say it is L.
- This LR will be the final answer of the cube root.

Example:– Find the cube root of 592704

Solution:– There will be 2 groups of numbers having 3 digits in each group. Here 592 and 704 are the two groups.

For unit digit 4 of the cube root we will have 4 at the unit place; hence R = 4 (Refer Table 10.1). For the second pair 592 we see that $8^3 < 592 < 9^3$; hence L = 8 (Refer Table 10.2).

$$\sqrt[3]{592 \ \ 704}$$
$$L = 8 \ \ R = 4$$

Hence, $(592704)^{1/3} = 84$

Example:– Find the cube root of 389017

Solution:– There will be 2 groups of number having 3 digits in each group. Here 389 and 017 are the two groups.

For Unit digit 7 of the cube root we will have 3 at the unit place; hence R = 3 (Refer Table 10.1). For the second pair 389 we see that $7^3 < 389 < 8^3$; hence L = 7 (Refer Table 10.2).

$$\sqrt[3]{\overset{|}{389}\ \overset{|}{017}}$$
$$L = 7\ R = 3$$

Hence, $(389017)^{1/3} = 73$

Example:– Find the cube root of 117649

Solution:– There will be 2 groups of number having 3 digits in each group. Here 117 and 649 are two groups.

For Unit digit 9 of the cube root we will have 9 at the unit place; hence R = 9 (Refer Table 10.1). For the second pair 117 we see that $4^3 < 117 < 5^3$; hence L = 4 (Refer Table 10.2).

$$\sqrt[3]{\overset{|}{117}\ \overset{|}{649}}$$
$$L = 4\ R = 9$$

Hence, $(117649)^{1/3} = 49$

Example:– Find the cube root of 238328

Solution:– Here 238 and 328 are two groups.

For Unit digit 8 of the cube root we will have 2 at the unit place; hence R = 2 (Refer Table 10.1). For the second pair 238 we see that $6^3 < 238 < 7^3$; hence L = 6 (Refer Table 10.2).

$$\sqrt[3]{\overset{|}{238}\ \overset{|}{328}}$$
$$L = 6\ R = 2$$

Hence, $(283328)^{1/3} = 67$

Cube Root of a Number Having 7, 8 or 9 Digits

Rule:–
- Cube root of such numbers will have 3 pairs hence the cube root will have 3 digits. The left most pair will give you the value of the digit at hundreds place. Say it is L. Refer Table 10.2 for L.
- The unit digit can be determined by noticing the unit

digit of the number. Say it is R. Table 10.1 will help you to determine the unit digit of the cube root.
- The middle digit (**M**) will have to be determined by using Casting out 11s method and with the help of Table 10.3.

Example:– Find the cube root of 76765625

Solution:– Group the number in 3 digits from left to right.

$$76\ 765\ 625$$

Since unit digit is 5 hence R = 5

Moreover, $4^3 < 76 < 5^3$ gives you the value of L and L = 4. For the middle digit of the cube root first find the value of the number using Casting out 11s method.

76765625 in Casting out 11s will convert into $5 - 2 + 6 - 5 + 6 - 7 + 6 - 7 = 23 - 21 = 2$. Now see the Casting out 11s table and find the number whose Casting out 11s value comes out to be 2 and you can see that it is 7.

Let the middle digit of cube root be M. Hence our cube root is 4 M 5 and the Casting out 11s value of 4 M 5 is $5 + 4 - M$.

Equate the value of Casting out nines and we get,

$9 - M = 7\ M = 2$

Hence $(7676525)^{1/3} = 425$

Example:– Find the cube root of 279726264

Solution:– Group the number in 3 digits from left to right.

$$279\ 726\ 264$$

Since unit digit is 4 hence R = 4

Moreover, $6^3 < 279 < 7^3$ gives you the value of L and L = 6. For the middle digit of the cube root first find the value of the number using Casting out 11s method.

279726264 in Casting out 11s will convert into $4 - 6 + 2 - 6 + 2 - 7 + 9 - 7 + 2 = 19 - 26 = -7$. In order to make it positive add 11. Hence the final value of Casting out 11s is $11 - 7 = 4$. Now see the Casting out 11s table and find the number whose Casting out 11s value comes out to be 4 and you can see that it is 5.

Let the middle digit of cube root be M. Hence our cube root is 6 M 4 and the Casting out 11s value of 6 M 4 is 6 + 4 − M.

Equate the value of casting out nines we get,

10 − M = 5 ⇒ M = 5

Hence $(279726264)^{1/3} = 654$

Example:– Find the cube root of 672 221 376

Solution:– Group the number in 3 digits from left to right.

$$672 \quad 221 \quad 376$$

Since unit digit is 6 hence R = 6

Moreover, $8^3 < 672 < 9^3$ gives you the value of L and L = 8. For the middle digit of the cube root first find the value of the number using Casting out 11s method.

672 221 376 in Casting out 11s will convert into 6 − 7 + 3 − 1 + 2 − 2 + 2 − 7 + 6 = 19 − 17 = 2. Now see the Casting out 11s table and find the number whose Casting out 11s value comes out to be 2 and you can see that it is 7.

Let the middle digit of cube root be M. Hence our cube root is 6 M 4 and the Casting out 11s value of 8 M 6 is 6 + 8 − M.

Equate the value of Casting out nines we get,

14 − M = 7 ⇒ M = 7

Hence $(672\ 221\ 376)^{1/3} = 876$

Cube Root of a Number Having More than 9 Digits

As discussed above that number having more than 9 digits will have 4 digits in its cube root. Now the question is how to convert this number in less than 9 digits number so that the previous method can be applied. The answer is very simple- Divide the number by 8 successively until you get a number which is either 9 digits long or lesser and once you get your dream number apply the previous mentioned rule and get the cube root of such numbers.

For the final result – Multiply the three digits answer you obtained by multiples of 2 for each successive division of 8.

Example:– Find the cube root of 43022168064

Solution:– Group the number in 3 digits from left to right.

$$4 \quad 302 \quad 216 \quad 810$$

Since there are 4 groups so divide successively with 8.

```
8  | 43022168064
8  | 5377771008
     672221376
```

Hence, $4302216810 = 8 \times 8 \times 672221376$

In the above example we have extracted the cube root of 672221376 that comes out to be 876.

$(43022168064)^{1}/_{3} = (8 \times 8 \times 672221376)^{1}/_{3} = 2 \times 2 \times 876 = 3504$

Since unit digit is 6 hence R = 6

Moreover, $8^3 < 672 < 9^3$ gives you the value of L and L = 8. For the middle digit of the cube root first find the value of the number using Casting out 11s method.

672 221 376 in Casting out 11s will convert into $6 - 7 + 3 - 1 + 2 - 2 + 2 - 7 + 6 = 19 - 17 = 2$. Now see the Casting out 11s table and find the number whose Casting out 11s value comes out to be 2 and you can see that it is 7.

Let the middle digit of cube root be M. Hence our cube root is 6 M 4 and the Casting out 11s value of 8 M 6 is 6 + 8 − M.

Equate the value of Casting out nines we get,

$14 - M = 7 \Rightarrow M = 7$

Hence $(672\ 221\ 376)^{1}/_{3} = 876$

This is now the time for you to practice to understand the concept in depth.

Find the cube root of the following numbers.

a) 6892　　b) 636056　　c) 314432　　d) 8365427
e) 1061208　f) 8489664　g) 143055667　h) 9800344

So far we have seen the cube root of a number having exact cube root. Let's now find the cube root of any number from 1-1000 which is not a perfect cube. This will be done through the method of approximation.

Approximation Method

Cube root of a number less than 1000 which is not a cubic number can be extracted by this formula. This rule is called Approximation method and many of you who have read Calculus might have done this question. The best part of this method is that you can do calculation in seconds if you have learnt the cube of first ten natural numbers.

Cube root to be extracted =
Nearest perfect cubic number $\pm \dfrac{\text{Deviation}}{3 \times (\text{Perfect cubic number})^2}$

Example:– Find the cube root of 128

Solution:– Nearest cubic number of 128 is 125 whose cube root is 5.

　　Deviation = 128 − 125 = 3

Hence, $(128)^{1/3} = \dfrac{5 + 3}{3 \times 5^2} = 5 + 0.04 = 5.04$

Example:– Find the cube root of 761

Solution:– Nearest cubic number of 761 is 729 whose cube root is 9.

　　Deviation = 761 − 729 = 32

Hence, $(761)^{1/3} = 9 + \dfrac{32}{3 \times 9^2} = 9 + 0.131 = 9.131$

Example:– Find the cube root of 214

Solution:– Nearest cubic number of 214 is 216 whose cube root is 6.

Deviation = 214 − 216 = −2

Hence, $(214)^{1/3} = \dfrac{6 - 2}{3 \times 6^2} = 6 + 0.018 = 5.982$

This method will give you approximate result so you can't compare it with the calculator's result. But the fact of the matter is that this is correct up to at least 2 decimal places and this serves our purpose.

Let's do some practice.

Find the cube of the following numbers:

a) 56 b) 76 c) 87 d) 124
e) 247 f) 421 g) 654 h) 1024
i) 765 j) 1229 k) 1095 l) 1924

I hope you have learnt the method of extracting cube root of any number whether it is a perfect cube or not, through a shortcut method which will be of immense help in competitive examination where speed play a vital role.

11

Finding Percentage in your Head

Percentage is merely a two place decimal without the decimal point shown. Per cent has its origin from the Latin word *per centum* meaning per hundred. It can best be defined as: a fraction whose denominator is 100 is called a percentage and the numerator of the fraction is called the rate per cent.

The importance of percentage can be estimated with the fact that whether you go to a Bank for taking a loan or go to a shopping mall for buying something, you always feel the importance of calculating percentage. Let's take some examples to understand the importance of per cent in daily life.

a) If the bank offers you an interest rate on home loan @10% per annum it simply means that you have to pay ₹10 per ₹100.
b) Suppose while reading a newspaper early in the morning you find an ad claiming that you will get 50% + 50% off on buying a pair of jeans and in the evening you rush to the shop in the hope that you will get a 100% discount on the jeans then you are really thinking the other way because you have miscalculated the discount percentage the company or shop is offering you.
c) We all know that in order to get 1st Division in School/College examination you need to acquire 60% marks of the total.

It is not all, in every competitive examination you appear; you encounter some problems on percentage directly or indirectly.

This altogether shows that it is an important tool in our life. Here I shall not deal with the typical problems asked in examination involving percentage which come in the form of Profit and Loss, Simple or Compound Interest etc. but I shall simply show you the way how you can calculate a simple percentage.

This clearly shows the importance of percentage. 1% of a number is 1/100 of the number; 15% of a number is 15/100 and so on. This reminds me of a question which is crucial in primary levels and is used to some extent in senior or competitive levels—what per cent one number is of other. Let me explain it before I move into the main discussion.

What Per cent Is One Number of Another?

Follow these simple steps and get the answer in your mind.

- Put the number that follows the word *what per cent is* in the numerator of the fraction
- Place the other number in the denominator of the fraction.
- Reduce the fraction to its simplest part if possible and finally multiply the result by 100.

Example:– What per cent is 16 of 80?

Solution:– Place 16 in numerator and 80 at denominator and multiply the fraction by 100.

$$\frac{\cancel{16}}{\cancel{80}} = \frac{1}{5}$$

$$= \frac{1}{5} \times \cancel{100}\,20$$

Example:– What per cent is 36 of 4?

Solution:– Place 36 at the numerator and 4 at the denominator and multiply the result by 100.

$$\frac{\cancel{36}^{\,9}}{\cancel{4}} \times 100 = 900$$

Let's learn some special techniques to find a certain percentage of a number. These methods will give you an edge calculating faster.

Finding 2½% of a Number

Suppose you are asked to find 2½% of a number you will simply convert it into a fraction and multiply the number by 5/2 and divide it by 100 but this will undoubtedly take a minute. Let's learn some simple tricks to do it in your mind.

1. Divide the number whose 2½% you are going to calculate by 4
2. Move decimal point one place to left

Hey, did you get the answer? Of course, YES. Isn't it super simple?
Let me take some examples to focus on its working.

Example:– Find 2½% of 86

Solution:– Divide 86 by 4; 86 ÷ 4 = 21.5
Move the decimal point one place to the left = 2.15
Hence, 86 × 2½% = 2.15

Example:– Find 2½% of 648

Solution:– Divide 648 by 4; 648 ÷ 4 = 162
Move the decimal point one place to the left = 16.2
Hence, 648 × 2½% = 16.2

Finding 5% of a Number

Let me ask you a simple question: are you comfortable dividing a number by 2? Your answer is a big YES. Finding 5% of a number is as simple as dividing a number by 2. Let's see how it works.

1. Divide the number by 2
2. Move the decimal point one place to the left

Example:– Find 5% of 850

Solution:– Divide 850 by 2; 850 ÷ 2 = 425
Move the decimal point one place to the left = 42.5
Hence, 850 × 5% = 42.5

Example:– Find 5% of 326

Solution:– Divide 326 by 2; 326 ÷ 2 = 163
Move the decimal point one place to the left = 16.3
Hence, 326 × 5% = 16.3

Finding 10% of a Number

Finding 10% of a number is a child's play. You follow the simple steps and get the answer in seconds.

1. Simply Move the decimal point one place to the left

Example:– Find 10% of 729

Solution:– Move the decimal point one place to the left = 72.9
Hence, 729 × 10% = 72.9

Example:– Find 10% of 2549

Solution:– Move the decimal point one place to the left = 254.9
Hence, 2549 × 10% = 254.9

Finding 15% of a Number

If I ask you to divide a number by 2 you will do it comfortably. If I then ask you to multiply the number by 3 then also you will get the answer correctly. Thats all you have to do in order to find 15% of a number. Follow the steps.

1. Divide the number by 2
2. Multiply the result obtained by 3
3. Move the decimal point one place to the left

Example:− Find 15% of 43

Solution:− Divide 43 by 2; $43 \div 2 = 21.5$
Multiply it by $3 = 21.5 \times 3 = 64.5$
Move the decimal point one place to the left = 6.45
Hence, $43 \times 15\% = 6.45$

Example:− Find 15% of 438

Solution:− Divide 483 by 2; $438 \div 2 = 219$
Multiply it by $3 = 219 \times 3 = 657$
Move the decimal point one place to the left = 65.7
Hence, $438 \times 15\% = 65.7$

Finding 20% of a Number

Follow the steps.

1. Divide the number by 5

Example:− Find 20% of 43

Solution:− Divide 43 by 5; $43 \div 5 = 8.6$
Hence, $43 \times 20\% = 8.6$

Example:− Find 20% of 348

Solution:− Divide 348 by 5; $348 \div 5 = 69.6$
Hence, $348 \times 20\% = 69.6$

Finding 25% of a Number

Follow the steps.

1. Divide the number by 4

Example:– Find 25% of 86

Solution:– Divide 86 by 4; 86 ÷ 4 = 21.5
Hence, 86 × 25% = 21.5

Example:– Find 25% of 484

Solution:– Divide 484 by 4; 484 ÷ 5 = 121
Hence, 484 × 25% = 121

Finding 33 1/3% of a Number

Follow the steps.

1. Divide the number by 3

Example:– Find $33\frac{1}{3}$% of 69

Solution:– Divide 69 by 3; 69 ÷ 3 = 23
Hence, 69 × $33\frac{1}{3}$% = 23

Example:– Find $33\frac{1}{3}$% of 921

Solution:– Divide 921 by 3; 921 ÷ 3 = 307
Hence, 921 × $33\frac{1}{3}$% = 307

Finding 40% of a Number

Follow the steps.

1. Multiply the number by 4
2. Move the decimal one point to the left

Example:– Find 40% of 24

Solution:– Multiply the number by 4: 24 × 4 = 96
Move the decimal one point to the left = 9.6
Hence, 24 × 40% = 9.6

Example:– Find 40% of 49

Solution:– Multiply the number by 4: 49 × 4 = 196
Move the decimal one point to the left = 19.6
Hence, 49 × 40 % = 19.6

Finding 45% of a Number

In order to find 45% of a number follow these steps.

1. Divide the number by 2
2. Multiply the result obtained by 9
3. Move the decimal point one place to the left

Example:– Find 45% of 36

Solution:– Divide 36 by 2; 36 ÷ 2 = 18
Multiply it by 9 = 18 × 9 = 162
Move the decimal point one place to the left = 16.2
Hence, 36 × 45% = 16.2

Example:– Find 45% of 640

Solution:– Divide 640 by 2; 640 ÷ 2 = 320
Multiply it by 9 = 320 × 9 = 2880
Move the decimal point one place to the left = 288
Hence, 460 × 45% = 288

Finding 50% of a Number

It is as simple as asking a Grade 7 student to read the table of 2. Simply divide the number whose 50% you want to find by 2 and you get the answer.

Example:– Find 50% of 630

Solution:– Divide 630 by 2: 630÷2 = 315

Example:– Find 50% of 6850

Solution:– Divide 6850 by 2: 6850÷2 = 3425

Finding 55% of a Number

Multiplying a number by 11 is very easy. In the chapters on multiplication I have described a simple rule to multiply any number by 11. Simply put two zeros (along both sides) with the number and keep adding from right to left to get the answer.

Example:– 112 × 11 = ?

Solution:– 0(112)0 = 0+1 / 1+1 / 1+2 / 2+0 = 1232

In order to find 55% of a number follow the steps.

1. Divide the number by 2
2. Multiply the result obtained by 11
3. Move the decimal point one place to the left

Example:– Find 55% of 36

Solution:– Divide 36 by 2; 36 ÷ 2 = 18
Multiply it by 11 = 18 × 11 = 198
Move decimal point one place to left = 19.8
Hence, 36 × 55% = 19.8

Example:– Find 55% of 580

Solution:– Divide 640 by 2; 580 ÷ 2 = 290
Multiply it by 11 = 290 × 11 = 3190
Move the decimal point one place to the left = 319
Hence, 460 × 55% = 319

Finding 60% of a Number

Getting 60% of total marks is important if you want to be in the first division in any school/ college examination. Jokes apart, the simple way to find the 60% of a number involves the following steps.

1. Multiply the number by 6

2. Move the decimal point one place to the left

Example:– Find 60% of 540

Solution:– Multiply the number by 6 = 540 × 6 = 3240
Move decimal point one place to left = 324
Hence, 540 × 60% = 324

Example:– Find 60% of 42

Solution:– Multiply the number by 6 = 42 × 6 = 252
Move decimal point one place to left = 25.2
Hence, 42 × 60% = 25.2

Finding 75% of a Number

75 is 3 times 25. As discussed earlier in order to find the 25% of a number you have to divide the number by 4. This is just the extension of the previous rule with the difference that you have to multiply it again by 3. Follow the steps.

1. Divide the number by 4
2. Multiply the result by 3

Example:– Find 75% of 28

Solution:– Divide the number by 4: 28÷4 = 7
Multiply the number by 3 = 7 × 3 = 21
Hence, 28 × 75% = 21

Example:– Find 75% of 756

Solution:– Divide the number by 4: 756÷4 = 189
Multiply the number by 3 = 189 × 3 = 567
Hence, 756 × 75% = 567

Finding $66^2/_3$% of a Number

In order to find $66^2/_3$% of a number you need to divide the number

Finding Percentage in your Head

by 3 and multiply the result by 2.

1. Divide the number by 3
2. Multiply the result by 2

Example:– Find $66^2/_3$ of 108

Solution:– Divide the number by 3: $108 \div 3 = 36$
Multiply the number by 2 = $36 \times 2 = 72$
Hence, $108 \times 66^2/_3\% = 72$

Example:– Find $66^2/_3$ of 45

Solution:– Divide the number by 3: $45 \div 3 = 15$
Multiply the number by 2 = $15 \times 2 = 30$
Hence, $108 \times 66^2/_3\% = 30$

Finding $16^2/_3\%$ of a Number

In order to find $16^2/_3\%$ of a number you need to simply divide the number by 6

1. Divide the result by 6

Example:– Find $16^2/_3$ of 108

Solution:– Divide the number by 6: $108 \div 6 = 18$
Hence, $108 \times 16^2/_3\% = 18$

Example:– Find $16^2/_3$ of 54

Solution:– Divide the number by 6: $54 \div 6 = 9$
Hence, $54 \times 16^2/_3\% = 9$

Hope you have enjoyed doing calculations with this new technique with great speed and accuracy. Initially you may face some discomfort doing this and remembering the rules but with a little practice you will get mastery over this. Let me put the above method in a tabular form which will help you to revise the whole chapter in a glance.

Percentage of a Number	Rule
2½	N /40
5	N /20
10	N /10
12½	N /8
$16^2/_3$	N /6
20	N /5
25	N /4
$33^1/_3$	N /3
50	N /2
$66^2/_3$	2N / 3
75	N − N /4
87½	N − N /8

Practice will help you understand the table better and you will be easily able to find the result faster and faster. So keep practising and attain mastery over the rule.

12

Doing Fractions Is so Much Fun

Introduction

A number expressed as quotient in the form of $\frac{N}{D}$ is called fraction.

Where N = Numerator and D = Denominator

The bottom number tells you how many parts something is divided into. It is interesting to note here that the denominator can never be equal to zero.

Suppose a pizza is divided into 4 parts or quarters then each part is one-fourth of the whole. This can be written as ¼.

Fractions are a form of division. The line of fraction means that you have to divide the upper number by the lower number.

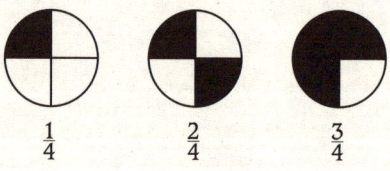

Figure 12.1

Types of Fractions

There are different types of fractions which we generally use. Some of them are discussed here for your convenience. It is interesting to know that in Egyptian mathematics a fraction with numerator 1 was known as Horus Fraction. You can see this interesting fraction in the picture below.

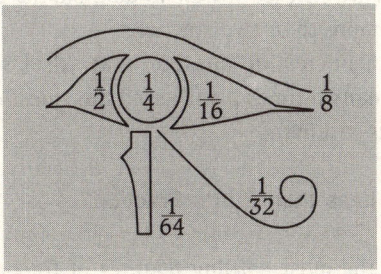

Figure 12.2: *Horus Eye Fraction*

A fraction with 1 as numerator is called **unit fraction**.

Example:– ½, ¼ etc.

A fraction having numerator less than its denominator is called **proper fraction**.

Example:– $5/11$, $14/26$ etc.

A fraction having denominator less than its numerator is called **improper fraction**.

Example:– $4/3$, $8/5$ etc.

A fraction with whole and a fractional part is called **mixed fraction**.

Example:– $4\tfrac{5}{7}$, $8\tfrac{2}{9}$

When the numerator and denominator of a fraction is changed inversely it is known as **inverse fraction**.

Example:– The inverse fraction of ¾ is 4/3

Fractions in which denominators are powers of 10 are known as **decimal fractions**.

Example:– 1/10

Operation on Fraction

In this chapter we will learn how to add, subtract, multiply and divide two or more than two fractions.

There is an interesting question that arises while handling fractions and many a times I was asked this question by students in mathematics seminars.

Why Is 2 × 2 Less than 2 in a Fraction?

This is one of the most baffling features of fractions that when you multiply the denominator by any positive integer the result will be less than the previous result.

$$1/_{2 \times 2} = 1/4 < 1/2$$

Mathematics is generally considered a difficult subject due to its complexity which sometimes creates problems for general readers. We are so accustomed to thinking of multiplication as an increasing process that we hardly accept the fact that it will lead to a decreasing process when we deal with the same in fractions.

Multiplication is obviously an increasing process if you count a number more than once. Let's understand it with the nursery table.

3 times 1 is 3   3 times 2 is 6   3 times 3 is 9...

But if you count a number less than once, as we do in fractions then obviously the result will be smaller than the previous one.

$1/_{2 \times 4} = 1/2 \times 1/4$ simply means that you are counting ½ exactly ¼ times. This clearly opens the Pandora's box of mathematical concepts. As long as you are multiplying a number with a number that is more than 1 you will get a larger value but when you start multiplying with a number less than one the result will be just the opposite.

Addition of Fractions

Addition of fractions is simple and you must have done it at the Upper Primary level itself. I shall take some cases which are common and generally asked in competitive examination and focus on that.

Case 1:– When the two fractions to add have numerator 1

Shortcut Formula:– $\dfrac{\text{Sum of the denominator}}{\text{Product of the denominator}}$

Example:– $1/5 + 1/6$

Solution:– Here the denominators are 5 and 6.
   Sum of the denominators = 5 + 6 = 11
   Product of the denominators = 5 × 6 = 30
   Hence, 1/5 + 1/6 = 11/30

Example:– $1/7 + 1/9$

Solution:– Here the denominators are 7 and 9.
   Sum of the denominators = 7 + 9 = 16
   Product of the denominators = 7 × 9 = 63
   Hence, 1/7 + 1/9 = 16/63

Case 2:– When two fractions have different denominators

This is a bit problematic as you have to convert each fraction into a fraction with equal denominator. But a simple mental exercise can help you to get the answer instantly. **This can be easily done by vertical and crosswise multiplication technique.**

Example: 5/7 + 4/5 = ?

Solution:– The crosswise operation is shown below

$$\dfrac{5}{7} \times\!\!+\!\!\times \dfrac{4}{5}$$

$$= \dfrac{25 + 28}{35} = \dfrac{53}{35}$$

Doing Fractions Is so Much Fun

Example:- 2/3 + 5/8 =?

Solution:- The crosswise operation is shown below

$$\frac{2}{3} \times \frac{+5}{8}$$

$$= \frac{16(2 \times 8) + 15(3 \times 5)}{24} = \frac{31}{24}$$

Example:- 7/11 + 2/9 =?

Solution:- The crosswise operation is shown below

$$\frac{7}{11} \times \frac{+2}{9}$$

$$= \frac{63(7 \times 9) + 22(2 \times 11)}{99} = \frac{85}{99}$$

Case 3:- Adding two fractions when denominators have common factors

Finding the answer of fractions when the denominators have common factors is a tough job in the traditional method as you will first find the Least Common Multiple (LCM) of the denominators and then convert both the fractions into fractions with a common denominator and follow the previous method. Let me explain here some thing different.

- Take the Highest Common Factor (HCF) of denominators.
- Divide the denominators with HCF and write down the quotient obtained below the corresponding denominator.
- For numerator cross-multiply the numerators with the quotient written below.
- For denominator cross-multiply either of the denominators with the quotient.

Example:– 5/18 + 4/27

Solution:–

$$\frac{5}{18} + \frac{4}{27}$$

$18 = 2 \times 9$ and $27 = 3 \times 9$

- Take the HCF of denominators, which is 9, and write the quotient below the denominator as shown here.

$$\frac{5}{18} \; \frac{+4}{27}$$
$$(2) \quad (3)$$

- Cross-multiply the numerator with the quotient as shown and write it as numerator.

$$\frac{5}{18} \diagdown \!\!\! \diagup \frac{+4}{27}$$
$$(2) \quad (3)$$

Numerator = $5 \times 3 + 4 \times 2 = 15 + 8 = 23$

- For denominator cross-multiply either of the denominators with the quotient.

$$\frac{5}{18} \diagdown \!\!\! \diagup \frac{+4}{27}$$
$$(2) \quad (3)$$

Denominator = $18 \times 3 = 54$ or $27 \times 2 = 54$

Hence, $\frac{5}{18} + \frac{4}{27} = \frac{23}{54}$

Case 4:– Adding more than two fractions

Addition of more than two fractions looks tough but it will be easy when you follow the given steps.

- Chose the fraction for which you want the operation. Circle its numerator
- Strike the number vertically and horizontally along with the number except itself
- Now multiply the left-out numbers
- Do the same operation for the rest of the fraction

- For denominator, multiply the denominator of all the fractions.

Example:– ¾ + ²/₃ + ²/₅

Solution:–

$$\frac{3}{4} + \frac{2}{3} + \frac{2}{5}$$

③ 2——2   3̶ ② 2   3—2 ②
4 3   5   4 3̶ 5   4 3 5̶

The pictorial representation above shows that for the first fraction all numbers in the horizontal line except the numerator of the first fraction have been struck and the vertical number below the concerned numerator is struck. The same is followed for the rest of the fractions.

For the first fraction whose numerator is 3, the numbers along the line in the other fractions like 2 and 2 are cut. Moreover, the number in the vertical line along with the numerator 3 is also struck out. Now the left-out numbers for the first fraction are—3, 3 and 5. Multiplying these numbers will give you the final result for the first fraction. The second and third will be calculated likewise.

Hence the result

$$= \frac{45 + 40 + 24}{60} = \frac{109}{60}$$

Hope the detailed description helped you. Let me give one more example for your convenience.

Example:– 5⅓ + 3¼ + 7½

Solution:– First we convert the mixed fractions. The problem will now look like

$$^{16}/_3 + ^{13}/_4 + ^{15}/_2$$

⑯   13——15   16   ⑬   15   16——13   ⑮
3   4   2   3   4   2   3   4   2
16 × 4 × 2 = 128   13 × 3 × 2 = 78   15 × 3 × 4 = 80

156 *Maths Made Easy*

Hence, Numerator = 128 + 78 + 180 = 386
Denominator = 3 × 4 × 2 = 24
Fraction = 386 / 24

Case 5:– Adding two mixed fractions

Rule:– Don't break the mixed fractions into improper fractions and add them separately. Instead, add the whole parts first and fractional part separately. If you find that the sum of fractional part can be further converted into mixed fraction, do it.

Example:– Add $2^3/_7 + 4^5/_7$

Solution:– Add the whole part first:– 2 + 4 = 6
Add the fractional part:– 3/7 + 5/7 = 8/7 = $1^1/_7$
Hence, $2^3/_7 + 4^5/_7 = 6 + 1^1/_7 = 7^1/_7$

Example:– Add $4^1/_2 + 3\ ^7/_9$

Solution:– Add the whole part first: 4 + 3 = 7
Add the fractional part:– $^1/_2 + ^7/_9 = \dfrac{1 \times 9 + 2 \times 7}{2 \times 9} = \dfrac{23}{18} = 1^5/_{18}$

Hence, $4^1/_2 + 3^7/_9 = 7 + 1^5/_{18} = 8^5/_{18}$

Subtraction of Fractions

If you are proficient in handling the addition of fractions easily, you can do the subtraction in the same effective way. Let me categorize the subtraction under different subtitles for your convenience.

Case 1:– When the two fractions to subtract have numerator 1

Shortcut Formula:– $\dfrac{\text{Difference of the denominator}}{\text{Product of the denominator}}$

Example:– $^1/_5 - ^1/_6$

Solution:– Here the denominators are 5 and 6.

Sum of the denominators = 6 − 5 = 1
Product of the denominators = 5 × 6 = 30
Hence, $1/5 - 1/6 = 1/30$

Example:- $1/7 - 1/9$

Solution:- Here the denominators are 7 and 9.
Sum of the denominators = 9 − 7 = 2
Product of the denominators = 7 × 9 = 63
Hence, $1/7 - 1/9 = 2/63$

Case 2: When the denominators are different

Subtraction of fractions can be done by cross-multiplication method quickly. The important point to remember is that while finding the numerator, the first number in subtraction will be the product of the numerator of first fraction and the denominator of the second fraction.

Example:- Solve $2/5 - 1/4$

Solution:-

$$\frac{2}{5} \diagdown \frac{1}{4}$$

$$= \frac{8-5}{20} = \frac{3}{20}$$

Example:- Solve $11/7 - 2/5$

Solution:- Numerator can be found by cross-multiplication method and denominator can be found by multiplying the denominators of each fractions.

$$\frac{11}{7} \diagdown \frac{2}{5}$$

$$\frac{11 \times 5 - 2 \times 7}{7 \times 5} = \frac{55-14}{35} = \frac{41}{35}$$

Example:- Solve $5/9 - 3/4$

Solution:– The subtraction of this fraction can be done easily in the same fashion. As I had told you earlier, in the case of subtraction we have to be a bit cautious and first write the product of numerator of first fraction and denominator of second fraction.

$$\frac{5}{9} - \frac{3}{4} = \frac{20-27}{36} = \frac{-7}{36}$$

Case 3:– Subtracting two mixed fractions

In case of mixed fractions, the operation on the whole part and fractional parts are done separately.

Example:– Solve $3^2/_7 - 1^1/_5$

Solution:– First do the operation with the whole part: $3 - 1 = 2$
Now subtract the fractional part as shown below

$$\frac{2}{7} - \frac{1}{5} = \frac{10-7}{35} = \frac{3}{35}$$

Hence, $3^2/_7 - 1^1/_5 = 2^3/_{35}$

Example:– Solve $5^2/_5 - 2^4/_7$

Solution:– Subtract the whole part first : $5 - 2 = 3$
Now it is the time to do the operation on fractional parts as shown here.

$$\frac{2}{5} - \frac{4}{7} = \frac{14-20}{35} = \frac{-4}{35}$$

Here the fractional part is negative. Don't worry, you can easily deal with this. Subtract the negative part from 1 which will diminish the whole part by 1.
New fractional part = $1 - ^4/_{35} = ^{31}/_{35}$
$5^2/_5 - 2^4/_7 = 2^{31}/_{35}$

Multiplication of Fractions

Multiplication of fractions is quite easy. To multiply fractions together, multiply the numerators and denominators of each fraction and place them rightly. Wherever possible try to simplify by reducing and cancelling.

Example:– Solve $\dfrac{2}{15} \times \dfrac{5}{12} \times \dfrac{10}{70}$

Solution:–

$$\dfrac{{}^1\cancel{2}}{{}_3\cancel{15}} \times \dfrac{{}^1\cancel{5}}{{}_6\cancel{12}} \times \dfrac{\cancel{10}}{\cancel{70}} = \dfrac{1}{126}$$

Example:– Solve $\dfrac{12}{21} \times \dfrac{8}{60} \times \dfrac{7}{5}$

Solution:–

$$\dfrac{{}^1\cancel{12}}{{}_3\cancel{15}} \times \dfrac{\cancel{8}}{{}_5\cancel{60}} \times \dfrac{\cancel{7}^1}{\cancel{5}} = \dfrac{8}{75}$$

As we have seen the multiplication of fractions is quite an easy job which is nothing but simplifying the fractions by breaking them into smaller fractions. These operations can be done better if you know the divisibility rules of different numbers which I shall describe in this chapter later. Let us now begin with some special cases.

1. To multiply a number by ¾

Rule:– (a) Divide the number by 4 and subtract the result from the number itself.

Explanation:– $1 - \frac{1}{4} = \frac{3}{4}$

Example:– $1848 \times \frac{3}{4}$

Solution:– $1848 \div 4 = 462$
and $1848 - 462 = 1386$

Rule:– (b) We know ½ + ¼ = ¾
and ½ × ½ = ¼

Now apply this logic to get the correct answer.

Halve the number two times successively and add the results.

1848 ÷ 2 = 924
924 ÷ 2 = 462
924 + 462 = 1386

Hence, 1848 × ¾ = 1386

Let's do some more problems for practice.

Example:– Solve 128 × ¾

Solution:– Halve the number two times successively and add the results.

128 ÷ 2 = 64
and
64 ÷ 2 = 32
Add both the results
64 + 32 = 96

Hence, 128 × ¾ = 96

2. To multiply a number by 2½

If you are asked to multiply a number by 2½ your first reaction will be to convert 2½ into a fraction and then solve it. I shall do something differently but still you will be able to easily understand it. Divide the number by 4 and put one zero at the end of the result obtained. You can also solve it in another way which is just a simplification of the method explained. Divide the number by 2 two times and put a zero at the end of the final result.

Example:– Multiply 36 by 2½

Solution:– Divide 36 by 4

36 ÷ 4 = 9

Now put a zero at the end of the result obtained.

Doing Fractions Is so Much Fun

Hence, 36 × 2½ = 90

Example:- Multiply 546 by 2½

Solution:- First put a zero after the number to be multiplied. This will make 546 as 5460. Now divide 5460 by 4
 5460 ÷ 4 = 1365
Hence, 546 × 2½ = 1365

3. Multiply two mixed numbers when they both end in ½ and the sum of their whole numbers is even

Rule:- a) Multiply the whole numbers
 b) Take the average of the whole numbers or divide the sum of whole numbers by 2
 c) Add both the results and attach ¼ at the end.

Example:- $8\frac{1}{2} \times 4\frac{1}{2}$

Solution:- Multiply the whole parts = 8 × 4 = 32
 Take average of 8 and 4 = (8 + 4)/2 = 6
 Add both the results = 32 + 6 = 38
 Attach ¼ with the previous result = 38¼

Hence, 8½ × 4½ = 38¼

Example:- 12½ × 8½

Solution:- Multiply the whole parts = 12 × 8 = 96
 Take average of 12 and 8 = (12 + 8) ÷ 2 = 10
 Add both the results = 96 + 10 = 106
 Attach ¼ with the previous result = 106¼

Hence, 12½ × 8½ = 106¼

4. Multiply two mixed numbers when they both end in ½ and the sum of the whole numbers is odd

Rule:- a) Multiply the whole numbers
 b) Take average of the whole numbers or divide the sum

of the whole numbers by 2 and drop the fractional part

c) Add both the results and attach ¾ at the end.

Example:– $7^1/_2 \times 4^1/_2$

Solution:– Multiply the whole parts = 7 × 4 = 28

Take average of 7 and 4 = (7 + 4)/2 = 5½

Add both the results by dropping the fractional part = 28 + 5 = 33

Attach ¾ to the previous result = 33¾

Hence, 7½ × 4½ = 33¾

Example:– 13½ × 8½

Solution:– Multiply the whole parts = 13 × 8 = 104

Take average of 13 and 8 = (13 + 8) ÷ 2 = 10½

Add both the results by dropping the fractional part = 104 + 10 = 114

Attach ¾ to the previous result = 114¾

Hence, 12½ × 8½ = 106¾

5. To multiply two mixed fractions having the same whole part and where the sum of the fractional parts is 1.

The fractional part should add up to 1. The fractional part can be these or any other combinations.

½ + ½ = 1
¼ + ¾
$1/_3 + 2/_3$
$1/_5 + 4/_5$

Rule:– a) Multiply the whole number by its next digit.
b) Multiply the fractional parts
c) Add the two to get the final result.

Example:– Multiply 13½ by 13½

Solution:– Multiply 13 by its next digit. 13 × 14 = 182
Multiply the fractional parts ½ × ½ = ¼
Add the two results = 182¼

Hence, 13½ × 13½ = 182¼

Example:– Multiply 18¼ by 18¾

Solution:– Multiply 18 by its next digit. 18 × 19 = 342
Multiply the fractional parts ¼ × ¾ = $3/16$
Add the two results = $342 \, 3/16$

Hence, 18¼ × 18¾ = $342 \, 3/16$

6. Multiply two mixed fractions

Multiplying two mixed fractions involves a lot of steps. We simply convert the mixed fraction into improper fractions and reduce the fractions into smallest fractions. But this is not the only way out. You can learn some better ways to handle the odd situation. Here we shall learn the technique to multiply two mixed fractions without converting it into improper fractions.

The whole process involves the use of distributive property.
A × (B + C) = A × B + A × C

Few years ago I was going through an article which had used the mnemonic FOIL to solve such multiplications. FOIL stands for First, Outer, Inner and Last term. Let's do the multiplication of mixed fractions.

Example:– Multiply 5½ by 4¼

Solution:– 5½ can be written as 5 + ½ and 4¼ can be written as 4 + ¼. Let's do the multiplication.

$$(5 + ½) \times (4 + ¼) = 5 \times 4 + 5 \times ¼ + 4 \times ½ + ½ \times ¼$$
$$= 20 + 5/4 + 2 + 1/8$$
$$= 20 + 1¼ + 2 + 1/8$$
$$= (20 + 1 + 2) + (1/4 + 1/8)$$
$$= 23 + 3/8 = 23\, 3/8$$

As you can see the above method involves a lot of steps, but it can be solved easily if you apply your mind well and convert the fractional part into decimal fraction.

$(5 + \frac{1}{2}) \times (4 + \frac{1}{4}) = 5.50 \times 4.25$

Can you do the multiplication by dot and stick method? We first do the multiplication and place the decimal after the result is obtained.

Example:– Multiply 550 by 425

Solution:–
Arrange the number on the dots as shown below.

```
5 5 0    5 5 0    5 5 0    5 5 0    5 5 0
○ ○ ○    ○ ○ ○    ○ ○ ○    ○ ○ ○    ○ ○ ○
○ ○ ○    ○ ○ ○    ○ ○ ○    ○ ○ ○    ○ ○ ○
4 2 5    4 2 5    4 2 5    4 2 5    4 2 5
  20       30       35       25        0
```

= 20 / 30 / 35 / 25 / 0

Hence, $5.50 \times 4.25 = 23.3750 = 23.375$

This clearly shows that fractions can be easily solved by converting them into decimal fractions.

Example:– Multiply $3^4/_7$ by $12^5/_8$

Solution:– Since we can't convert the fractional part 4/7 into a terminating decimal fraction, it is advisable to convert both the mixed fractions into improper fractions.

$$3^4/_7 \times 12^5/_8 = 25/7 \times 101/8 = \frac{25 \times 101}{7 \times 8} = \frac{2525}{56}$$

Division of a Fraction

Division of a fraction is simple provided you understand these basic concepts:

Doing Fractions Is so Much Fun

a) $x \div y/z = xz/y$
b) $x/y \div z = x/yz$
c) $x/y \div p/q = xq/yp$

The above concept simply asks to invert the second part and proceed as in multiplication.

Let's do some examples on division.

Example:– Divide $4^5/_8$ by $3^1/_6$

Solution:– Convert the two mixed fractions into improper fractions. They will turn into 37/8 and 19/6 respectively. Since this is a division, the rule discussed above tells us to turn the divider upside down and handle it as multiplication.

$$4^5/_8 \div 3^1/_6 = 37/8 \times 6/19$$

$$= \frac{37}{\cancel{8}_4} \times \frac{\cancel{6}^3}{19} = \frac{111}{76}$$

Example:– Divide 3/16 by 2

Solution:– $^3/_{16} \div ^2/_1 = ^3/_{16} \times ^1/_2 = ^3/_{32}$

Case 1:– If the denominators of fractions are the same

Rule:– Ignore the denominator and simply divide the numerators

Example:– Divide $^4/_7$ by $^2/_7$

Solution:– As you can see here the fractions have a common denominator. In such situations you can ignore the denominators and divide the numerators like whole numbers.

$^4/_7 \div ^2/_7 = 4 \div 2 = 2$

Example:– Divide $4^6/_8$ by $2^3/_8$

Solution:– First convert the mixed fractions into improper fractions. You can see 38/8 and 19/8 as improper fractions. Since the denominators are same so we can ignore the denominators and handle the situation easily.

$$4^6/_8 \div 2^3/_8 = {}^{38}/_8 \div {}^{19}/_8 = 38 \div 19 = 2$$

Case 2:– Divide a number by ½
To get rid of the fractional part, double both parts and divide.

Example:– Divide 14 by 3½

Solution:– $14 \div 3½ = 28 \div 7 = 4$

Example:– Divide 49 by 5½

Solution:– $49 \div 5½ = 98 \div 11 = 8^{10}/_{11}$

Comparing Fractions

Sometimes we need to compare two fractions or arrange them into ascending or descending order. We shall learn the simplest method to handle this situation.

Rule:– If you have to compare two fractions then multiply the numerator of the first by the denominator of the second fraction and vice versa. In simple words, cross-multiply the fractions and check which one is greater or smaller. Let's take some examples to understand the concepts.

Example:– Which one is larger—2/11 or 9/13?

Solution:–

$$\frac{2}{11} \text{ and } \frac{9}{13}$$

After cross multiplication we get, $2 \times 13 = 26$ and $9 \times 11 = 99$. Now the question is which one is greater, 26 or 99. Absolutely $26 < 99$. Hence

$$\frac{2}{11} < \frac{9}{13}$$

Example:– Compare 7/8 and 5/6

Solution:– Cross multiply the fractions as shown above and directed by the rule.

7 × 6 = 42 and 5 × 8 = 40

This clearly shows 42 is greater than 40. Hence,

$$\frac{7}{8} < \frac{5}{6}$$

Arranging in Ascending and Descending Order

In many competitive examinations you are asked to compare a set of fractions and arrange them in ascending or descending order. The general rule which we adopt is to take the LCM of denominators and make denominators of each fraction equal and compare them. Let's see how it works.

Example:– Arrange the following fractions in ascending order

$$\frac{7}{8}, \frac{2}{3}, \frac{5}{6}$$

Solution:– Take the LCM of 8, 3 and 6 which is 24. Make the denominator of each fraction 24 by multiplying with an equal number.

$$\frac{7 \times 3}{8 \times 3} = \frac{21}{24} \qquad \frac{2 \times 8}{3 \times 8} = \frac{16}{24} \qquad \frac{5 \times 4}{6 \times 4} = \frac{20}{24}$$

As we can see that denominators of each fractions are equal hence the ascending or descending order can be arranged by looking at the numerator.

$$\frac{21}{24} > \frac{20}{24} > \frac{16}{24}$$

$$\frac{7}{8} > \frac{5}{6} > \frac{2}{3}$$

But the method explained above is time consuming, isn't it?

Let's do something new. You can also compare the fractions as shown below.

Example:– Arrange the following fractions in ascending order

$$\frac{7}{8} > \frac{2}{3} > \frac{5}{6}$$

Solution:– First compare the fractions 7/8 and 2/3 by cross multiplication method.

Again compare the fractions 2/3 and 5/6 by cross multiplication method.

$2 \times 6 < 3 \times 5$

so $\frac{2}{3} < \frac{5}{6}$

Finally compare the fractions 7/8 and 5/6.

$7 \times 6 > 5 \times 8$

Hence, $\frac{7}{8} > \frac{5}{6}$

Now you can arrange the above three fractions in ascending order

$$\frac{2}{3} < \frac{5}{6} < \frac{7}{8}$$

But this method also takes a lot of time. Let's do something extraordinary so that we get the result faster, in a moment, without doing much calculation.

Follow the rule first and see the change.

Rule:– a) Find the difference of numerator and denominator
b) Now divide numerator of every fraction by the difference obtained
c) The greatest result obtained will have the greatest fraction and the least the smallest fraction

Example:– Arrange the following fractions in ascending order

$\frac{7}{8}, \frac{5}{6}, \frac{6}{9}, \frac{12}{13}$

Solution:– Find the difference of numerator and denominator of each fractions.

$8 - 7 = 1$
$6 - 5 = 1$
$9 - 6 = 3$
$13 - 12 = 1$

Now divide the numerator of each fractions by the difference of numerator and denominator.

$7 \div 1 = 7$
$5 \div 1 = 5$
$6 \div 3 = 2$
$12 \div 1 = 12$

Since, 12 is the greatest number and 2 is the smallest number hence 12/13 is the greatest number and 6/9 is the smallest fraction.

Rule:– In the following fraction

$$\frac{x}{a}, \frac{x+a}{y+b}, \frac{x+2a}{y+2b} \ldots \frac{x+na}{y+nb}$$

If $a > b$ then,

$\frac{x+na}{y+nb}$ is the greatest and $\frac{x}{a}$ is the smallest

If the difference between numerator and denominator is the same and fractions are in ascending order then the 1st fraction is the smallest one and the last fraction is the greatest one.

Example:– In 7/8, 8/9 and 9/10; 7/8 is the smallest and 9/10 is the greatest.

You can do a better trick with patience and practice. Hope you have understood the core of fractions and have enjoyed it. The only mantra of success is practice and persistence so take a lot of examples and practise them.

13

Trigonometry Is No More Tiring

Introduction

Trigonometry is a branch of mathematics which basically deals with the relation of all the three sides of a right angle triangle. The first thing that comes to our mind when we talk about a right angle triangle is—the Pythagorean triangle. The first reference to Pythagoras' triangle was found to be in the *Katyayana Sulbasutra* written in about 200 BC. In earlier days, in India people used to perform yagnas and for that the rishis used to prepare the altar in different shapes using the triplets now popularly known as Pythagorean Triplets.

As far as its discovery is concerned trigonometry was first discovered by the Greeks to aid in the study of astronomy. The Babylonians established the measurement of angles in degrees, minutes and seconds. From Hipparchus to Ptolemy to Aryabhata, all contributed to the development of trigonometry. There are six trigonometric ratios namely—**Sine**, **Cos** (ine), **Tan** (gent), **Cot** (angent), **Sec** (ant) and **Cosec** (ant).

Every trigonometric ratio shows a different relation between two of the three sides of a right angle triangle.

Let me remind you of the following concepts of trigonometry, which you have learnt at the secondary level. In a right angle triangle ABC with angle C = 90°, the various trigonometric ratios are defined as follows:—

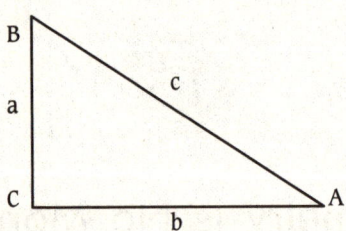

$$\text{Sin A} = \frac{\text{Perpendicular}}{\text{Hypotenuse}} \qquad \text{Cosec A} = \frac{\text{Hypotenuse}}{\text{Perpendicular}}$$

$$\text{Cos A} = \frac{\text{Base}}{\text{Hypotenuse}} \qquad \text{Sec A} = \frac{\text{Hypotenuse}}{\text{Base}}$$

$$\text{Tan A} = \frac{\text{Perpendicular}}{\text{Base}} \qquad \text{Cot A} = \frac{\text{Base}}{\text{Perpendicular}}$$

How to Learn the Mnemonics for Trigonometric Values?

There are many mnemonics which will help you to learn the trigonometric ratios of an angle in no time. I shall focus here on two of them—one which is more sophisticated and one which has been used commonly in Indian schools for long.

- **S**ome **P**eople **H**ave **C**urly **B**rown **H**air **T**owards **P**ulled **B**ack—Here the bold letters shows the trigonometric relations. S stands for Sin, C stands for Cos and T stands for Tan whereas P stands for Perpendicular, B stands for Base and H stands for Hypotenuse. This single line helps you to understand the relations of sides in different trigonometric ratios.
  Sin A = P/H   Cos A = B/H   Tan A = P/B
- Let's learn a very funny mnemonic which will help you directly find the relation between two sides. The mnemonic is—**Pandit Badri Prasad Hari Hari Bole**. Let me explain it.

Sin	Cos	Tan
Pandit	Badri	Prasad
Hari	Hari	Bole
Cosec	Sec	Cot

Here, Sin A = P/H, Cos A = B/H and Tan A = P/B where P = Perpendicular, B = Base and H = Hypotenuse

How to Learn the Trigonometric Angles from 0 to 90?

After learning the relations of sides of a right angle triangle you must learn the value of angles for different ratios in trigonometry. The trigonometric angles will help you understand the application of trigonometry in general life. The slope of an angle, the elevation and depression angle are all based on the values of angles in different ratios.

First let me illustrate to you a table and later explain how you can construct that table or find out the values with the help of your fingers.

Ratio/Angle	0	30	45	60	90
Sin	0	½	$1/\sqrt{2}$	$\sqrt{3}/2$	1
Cos	1	$\sqrt{3}/2$	$1/\sqrt{2}$	½	0
Tan	0	$1/\sqrt{3}$	1	$\sqrt{3}$	Not defined
Cot	Not defined	$\sqrt{3}$	1	$1/\sqrt{3}$	0
Sec	1	$2/\sqrt{3}$	$\sqrt{2}$	2	Not defined
Cosec	Not defined	2	$\sqrt{2}$	$\sqrt{3}/2$	1

In the first look it seems that it is tough to learn this table but you can have it at your fingertips with a little practice and there will be absolutely no need to learn such a table at all.

Angles at your fingertips

In multiplication we have also seen the magic of our hands and learnt some basic multiplication techniques. Here we will see how helpful our hands are in memorizing the trigonometric table without pen and paper.

- Mark your fingers with angles from 0 to 90 as shown in the first figure.
- The number of fingers to the right of the designated angle finger will help you to find the value of **Cosine** whereas the number of fingers to the left part of the designated finger will help you to find the value of **Sine**.
- In picture 2, place the number of fingers on either on the right side of the designated angle finger to find the value of **Cosine** or number of fingers on the left side to find the value of **Sine**.

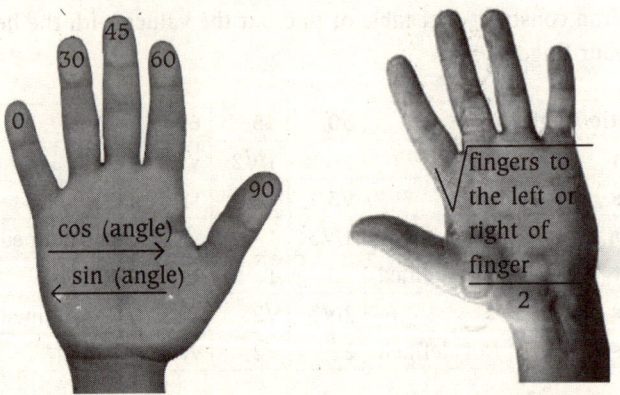

Figure 13.1　　　　　**Figure 13.2**

Working Method

You will be astonished to know that these fingers will help you find the value of the designated angle for both sine and cosine simultaneously. Suppose you have to find the value of Sin 30 and Cos 30, you can find both of these values in seconds.

- Bend the finger marked with 30 as shown here. Though it is not necessary but it is recommended if using this method for the first time as it will make your calculation flawless.

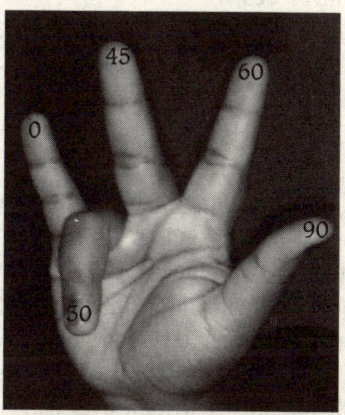

Figure 13.3

- Count the number of fingers to the right and left of the bent finger marked with angle 30.
  Fingers to the left of bent finger = 1
  Fingers to the right of bent finger = 3
- Cos 30 = √3/2 and Sin 30 = √1/2 = ½

Isn't it an easy method to find the value of different angles of sine and cosine simultaneously? Suppose you have to find the value of

Sin 45 = ?   Cos 45 = ?

Simply bend the finger with 45 marked on it. Count the number of fingers to the left or right of it. Place these values in square root and divide the result by 2.

Fingers to the left of bent finger = 2
Fingers to the right of bent finger = 2

Hence, Sin 45 = √2/ 2 = 1/√2
Cos 45 = √2/ 2 = 1/√2

We know that the tangent of an angle can be found by simply dividing the ratio of Sin and Cosine.

Tan A = Sin A / Cos A
Tan 30 = Sin30/ Cos30 = ½ / √3/2 = 1/√3

Moreover,
Sec A = 1/ Cos A   so   Sec 30 = 2/√3
Cosec A = 1/ Sin A   so   Cosec 30 = 2/1 = 2

I was teaching this technique of extracting trigonometric table for different angles of Sinθ and Cosθ in a DAV school in Bihar a few months ago when a student asked me how to extract the value of Tanθ and Cotθ with the help of finger technique. I then decided to extend the finger technique of extracting angles for different trigonometric ratios in my book. Let's see the following two images with the angles written over it.

Tan θ = Square root (Fingers to the left to bent finger/ finger to the right to the bent finger)

Cot θ = Square root (Fingers to the right to the bent finger/ finger to the left to the bent finger)

It means that you can work simultaneously to find the value of the Tan and Cot of any angle from 0 to 90 degrees. In the figure 3, finger indicating 30 degree has been bent. You can see that there is 1 finger to the left of bent finger and 3 fingers to the right side.

Hence, Tan 30 = 1/ √3 and Cot 30 = √3/1 = √3

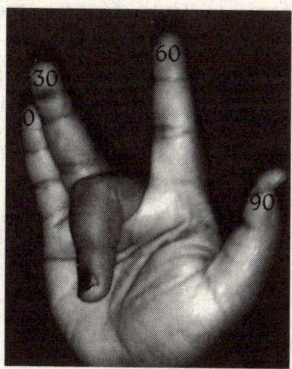

Figure 13.4

In Figure 4, finger with angle 45 marked on it has been bent. As you can see in the picture there are equal numbers of fingers on both sides of the bent finger.

Hence, Tan 45 = square root of (2/2) = 1

Cot 45 = square root of (2/2) = 1

I do hope you can learn the trigonometric table of different angles with the help of the above technique in no time. Even in the examination hall you can use this technique in case you forget a particular value. Try to practise it more and more so that you can learn the value automatically of different angles for different trigonometric ratios.

Practice Problem

a) Sin 60 = ?   b) Sec 45 = ?   c) Cot 90 = ?
d) Tan 45 = ?   e) Cos 60 = ?   f) Cosec 45 = ?

Angles in Different Quadrants

After learning the values of 0 to 90 for different trigonometric ratios, we should learn their extensions. The following mnemonic will help you find the values of any trigonometric ratio from 0 to 360 in no time.

Add Sugar To Coffee:– In Trigonometry, students of class 11 feel uneasy when they are asked to remember the Trigonometric Table for angles above 90 degrees but this one-line mnemonic **Add Sugar To Coffee** will certainly help you find the value of trigonometric value of any degree. Let's see how it works.

Add = ALL	Sugar = Sine/ Cosec
$\pi - \theta$	(I) $\pi/2 - \theta$
$\pi/2 + \theta$ (II)	$2n\pi + \theta$
To = Tan / Cot	Coffee = Cos / Sec
$\pi + \theta$	$3/2\, \pi + \theta$
$3/2\, \pi - \theta$ (III)	(IV) $2\pi - \theta$

The above representation will help you find the value of angles from 0 degree to 360 degrees and more. The only point to remember is that:

a) For $90 \pm \theta$, $270 \pm \theta$, trigonometric function changes into $Sin\theta \leftrightarrow Cos\theta$, $Tan\theta \leftrightarrow Cot\theta$ and $Sec\theta \leftrightarrow Cosec\theta$

b) For $180 \pm \theta$, $360 \pm \theta$, there will be no change in the result. Let us understand it more clearly.

In 1st Quadrant

In the first quadrant the angle should be less than 90 degrees and as discussed above for values less than 90 the trigonometric function changes to its complementary trigonometric function. Hence

Sin $(90 - \theta)$ = Cosθ
Cos $(90 - \theta)$ = Sinθ
Tan $(90 - \theta)$ = Cotθ
and so on.

For Second Quadrant

In second quadrant the value should be either $90 + \theta$ or $180 - \theta$ and the value of **Sine** will remain positive and so will be with its reciprocal **Cosec**. For the rest of the trigonometric ratios the result will bear a negative sign. I have discussed above that for $180 \pm \theta$ and $360 \pm \theta$ the trigonometric ratios will remain unchanged so let's see how the values of trigonometric ratios change for certain degrees in the 2nd quadrant.

$\mathrm{Sin}\,(90+\theta) = \mathrm{Cos}\theta$ $\mathrm{Sin}\,(180-\theta) = \mathrm{Sin}\theta$
$\mathrm{Cos}\,(90+\theta) = -\mathrm{Sin}\theta$ $\mathrm{Cos}\,(180-\theta) = -\mathrm{Sin}\theta$
$\mathrm{Tan}\,(90+\theta) = -\mathrm{Cot}\theta$ $\mathrm{Tan}\,(180-\theta) = -\mathrm{Tan}\theta$

I do hope the reader will enjoy the method and take the initiative to find the value of trigonometric function in the 3rd and 4th quadrants.

The above discussions can be easily understood through the following diagram.

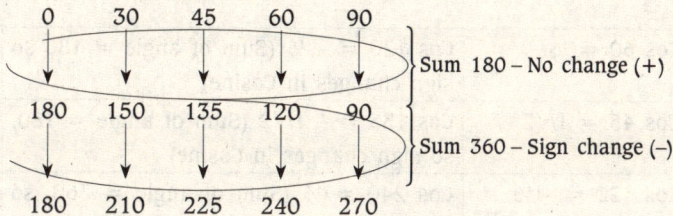

Diagram for value of SINE of an angle

Illustration

Sin 30 = ½ = Sin 150 (Sum of angles is 180, hence no sign change in result)
Sin 150 = ½ but Sin 210 = – ½ (Sum of angles is 360, hence negative sign in result)

Sin 60 = √3/2 = Sin 120 (Sum of angles is 180, hence no sign change in result)

Sin 120 = √3/2 but Sin 240 = -√3/2 (Sum of angles is 360, hence negative sign in result)

Let's now move the discussion to find the value of Cosine.

The above discussion can be easily understood through the following diagram.

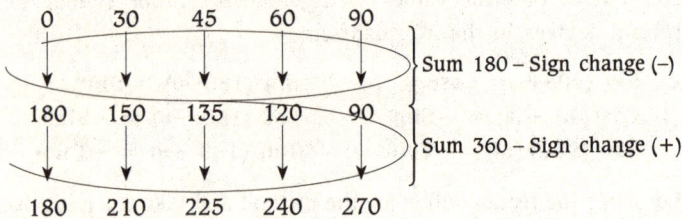

Diagram for value of COSINE of an angle

Illustration

Cos 60 = ½	Cos 120 = – ½ (Sum of angle = 180 so sign changes in Cosine)
Cos 45 = 1/√2	Cos 135 = – 1/√2 (Sum of angle = 180, so sign changes in Cosine)
Cos 120 = – ½	Cos 240 = ½ (Sum of angle = 360, so sign changes in Cosine)
Cos 135 = – 1/√2	Cos 225 = 1 / √2 (Sum of angle = 360, so sign changes in Cosine)

After we learn the trigonometric ratios and trigonometric values of different angles, we will now learn about triplets. Triplets help us find the trigonometric ratios in fraction of minutes. We shall also discuss here the method to find the triplets.

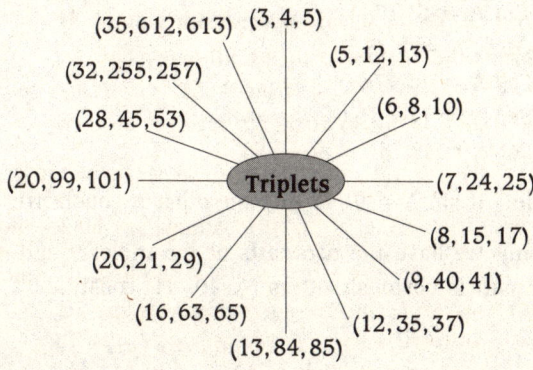

Figure 13.5

Triplet Chart

Let's see how triplets help you find the trigonometric ratios, sum and difference of two angles, double angles, triple angles and half angles. In addition to that, triplets help us to find the values of angles more than 90 degrees which we have discussed above.

If ABC be a right angle triangle with its side a, b and c and angle C = 90 then

TRIGONOMETRIC RATIO	VALUE	TRIPLET CASE
Sin A	a/c	1st value / 3rd value
Cos A	b/c	2nd value / 3rd value
Tan A	a/b	1st value / 2nd value
Cot A	b/a	2nd value / 1st value
Sec A	c/b	3rd value / 2nd value
Cosec A	c/a	3rd value / 1st value

Example:– If Tan A = 8 /15, find the value of other trigonometric ratios?

Solution:– We know that Tan A = Perpendicular /Base. For Tan A = 8/15, we have the following triplet

$$a = 8 \quad b = 15 \quad c = 17$$

Hence, Sin A = 8/17
   Cosec A = 17/8
   Cos A = 15/17
   Sec A = 17/15
   Cot A = 15/8

Example:– If sin A = 9/41 find the other trigonometric ratios?

Solution:– We have the two parts of the triplet 9 and 41. The missing part is obviously 40 as (9, 40, 41) constitute a triplet.

Hence,
$$a = 9 \quad b = 40 \quad c = 41$$

Now we have all the sides of a right angle triangle so it is now easy to find the rest of the trigonometric ratios.

   Cos A = 40/41
   Sec A = 41/40
   Tan A = 9/40
   Cot A = 40/9
   Cosec A = 41/9

I do hope you have enjoyed finding the trigonometric ratios without doing much calculation. This is the beauty of a triplet which lets you solve a problem in a fraction of minute.

Now this is time to do some practice.

a) Sin A = 7/25 find the other trigonometric ratios.
b) Tan A = 33/56, find the other trigonometric ratios.
c) Sec A = 5/4, find the other trigonometric ratios.

Sum of Angles Using Triplets

The following two formulae will help us find the sum of angles in trigonometry.

Sin (A + B) = Sin A Cos B + Cos A Sin B

$\cos(A + B) = \cos A \cos B - \sin A \sin B$

The main area of concern of using this formula is that if we are given

If $\sin A = 8/17$ and $\cos B = 3/5$, find the value of $\sin(A + B)$ and $\cos(A + B)$?

We have to first find the values of Cos A and Sin B and then substitute them in the above formula and then only after some calculation will we be able to get the answer. But if you remember the triplets then it will hardly take a minute to find the value of Sin (A + B) and Cos (A + B).

If the triplets of angle A are x, y, z and triplets for B are X, Y and Z, then the triplets for the angle A+B are given by:–

A	x	y	z
B	X	Y	Z
A + B	yX + xY	yY − xX	zZ

This can be better understood using the dot and cross method.

Example:– If Sin A = 3/5 and Sin B = 8/17, then find the value of Sin (A+B) and Cos (A+B)

Solution:– Let us first draw the triplet table for the angles A and B

A	3	4	5
B	8	15	17
A + B	3 × 15 + 4 × 8 = 77	4 × 15 − 3 × 8 = 36	5 × 17 = 85

Hence, Sin (A+ B) = 77/85
Cos (A + B) = 36/85

Example:– If Sin A = 7/25 and Sin B = 8/17 then find the value of Sin (A+B) and Cos (A+B)

Solution:– Let us first draw the triplet table for the angle A and B

A	7	24	25
B	8	15	17
A + B	7 × 15 + 24 × 8 = 297	24 × 15 – 7 × 8 = 304	25 × 17 = 425

Hence, Sin (A+ B) = 297/425
  Cos (A + B) = 304/425

Difference of Angles using Triplets

If the triplets of angle A are x, y, z and triplets for B are X, Y and Z then the triplet for the angle A+B are given by:–

A	x	y	z
B	X	Y	Z
A – B	xY – Xy	xX + yY	zZ

This can be better understood using the dot and cross method.

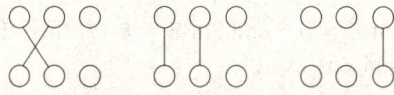

Example:– If Sin A = 7/25 and Sin B = 8/17 then find the value of Sin (A–B) and Cos (A–B)

Solution:– Let us first draw the triplets table for the angle A and B

A	7	24	25
B	8	15	17
A + B	7 × 15 – 24 × 8 = –77	24 × 15 + 7 × 8 = 416	25 × 17 = 425

Hence, Sin (A − B) = −77/425
Cos (A − B) = 416/425

If triplets have a negative sign then obviously the angle is obtuse.

Example:– If Sin A = 3/5 and Sin B = 8/17 then find the value of Sin (A−B) and Cos (A−B)?

Solution:– Let us first draw the triplets table for the angle A and B

A	3	4	5
B	8	15	17
A−B	3 × 15 − 4 × 8 = 13	4 × 15 + 3 × 8 = 84	5 × 17 = 85

Hence, Sin (A− B) = 13/85
Cos (A − B) = 84/85

Finding Trigonometric Angle using Triplets

If you know the exact triplets then you can find the triplets corresponding to sum/ difference of complementary/ supplementary triplets. Before we proceed to find the angle of (90 ± A) or (180 ± A) I would advise you to learn the triplets for 90, 180, 270 and 360:

Triplets for 90 = (1, 0, 1)
Triplets for 180 = (0, -1, 1)
Triplets for 270 = (-1, 0, 1)
Triplets for 360 = (0, 1, 1)

You can remember these triplets with the help of this circular diagram where one value is the image of another.

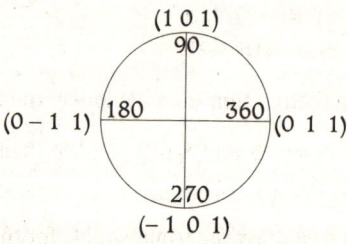

Let's see how we can compute the supplementary, complementary or reflex angles using triplets?

Triplets for 90 + A, 180 + A, 270 + A and 360 + A

Example:– If Sin A = 4/5, find the value of Sin (90 + A), Cos (90 + A) and Tan (90 + A)?

Solution:– Let's first put the triplet in order for angle A and 90. We know 3, 4, 5 is a triplet so for Sin A = 4/5, the missing triplet is obviously 3. Arrange the triplet accordingly.

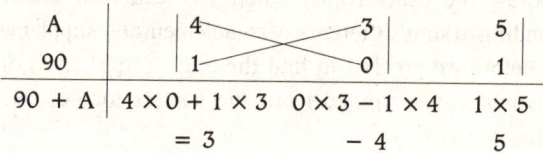

Hence, Sin (90 + A) = 3/5
Cos (90 + A) = −4/5
Tan (90 + A) = 3/−4

Example:– If tan A = 8/15, find the value of Sin (90 + A), Cos (90 + A) and Tan (90 + A)?

Solution:– Let's first put the triplet in order for angle A and 90. We know 8, 15, 17 is a triplet so for Tan A = 8/15, the missing triplet is obviously 17. Arrange the triplet accordingly.

A	8	15	17
90	1	0	1
90 + A	$8 \times 0 + 1 \times 15$	$0 \times 15 - 1 \times 8$	1×17
	= 15	− 8	17

Hence, Sin (90 + A) = 15/17
Cos (90+A) = −8/17
Tan (90+A) = 15/−8

Example:– If Sin A = 4/ 5, find the value of Sin (180 + A), Cos (180 + A) and Tan (180 + A)?

Solution:– Arrange the triplet accordingly.

A	4	3	5
180	0	−1	1
180 + A	$4 \times -1 + 0 \times 3$	$-1 \times 3 - 4 \times 0$	1×5
	= −4	− 3	5

Hence, Sin (180 + A) = −4/5
Cos (180+A) = −3/5
Tan (180+A) = −4 / −3 = 4/3

Example:– If Sin A = 4/ 5, find the value of Sin (270 + A), Cos (270 + A) and Tan (270 + A)?

Solution:– Arrange the triplet accordingly.

A	4	3	5
270	−1	0	1
270 + A	$4 \times 0 - 1 \times 3$	$0 \times 3 - 1 \times -4$	1×5
	= −3	4	5

Hence, Sin (270 + A) = −3/5
Cos (270+A) = 4/5
Tan (270+A) = −3/4

Example:– If Tan A = 8/15, find the value of Sin (360 + A), Cos (360 + A) and Tan (360 + A)?

Solution:– Arrange the triplet accordingly.

A	8 15	17
360	0 1	1
360 + A	8 × 1 + 0 × 15 1 × 15 − 0 × 8 1 × 17	
	= 8 15 17	

Hence, Sin (360 + A) = 8/17
Cos (360+A) = 15/17
Tan (360+A) = 8/15

Triplets for 90 −A, 180 − A, 270 −A and 360−A

Example:– If Sin A = 7/25, find the value of Sin (90 − A), Cos (90 − A) and Tan (90 − A)?

Solution:– Let's first put the triplet in order for angle A and 90. We know 7, 24, 25 is a triplet so for Sin A = 7/25, the missing triplet is obviously 24. Arrange the triplet accordingly.

90	1 0	1
A	7 24	25
90 − A	1 × 24 − 0 × 7 0 × 24 + 1 × 7 1 × 25	
	= 24 7 25	

Sin (90 − A) = 24/25
Cos (90 − A) = 7/25
Tan (90 − A) = 24/25

Example:– If Tan A = 9/40, find the value of Sin (180 − A), Cos (180 − A) and Tan (180 − A)?

Solution:– Let's first put the triplets in order for angle A and 90. We know 9, 40, 41 is a triplet so for Tan A = 9/40, the missing triplet is obviously 41. Arrange the triplet accordingly.

180	0 ⤫ −1	1
A	9 ⤫ 40	41
180 − A	0 × 40 −(−1) × 9 −1 × 40 + 0 × 9	1 × 41
	= 9 −40	41

Sin (180 − A) = 9/41
Cos (180 − A) = −40/41
Tan (180 − A) = −40/9

Example:− If Sin A = 7/25, find the value of Sin (270 − A), Cos (270 − A) and Tan (270 − A)?

Solution:− Arrange the triplets accordingly.

270	−1 ⤫ 0	1
A	7 ⤫ 24	25
270 − A	−1 × 24 − 0 × 7 0 × 24 + (−1) × 7	1 × 25
	= −24 − 7	25

Sin (270 − A) = −24/25
Cos (270 − A) = −7/25
Tan (270 − A) = −24/−7 = 24/7

Example:− If Tan A = 8/15, find the value of Sin (360 − A), Cos (360 − A) and Tan (360 − A)?

Solution:− Arrange the triplets accordingly.

360	0 ⤫ 1	1
A	8 ⤫ 15	17
360 − A	0 × 15 − 8 × 1 1 × 15 + 0 × 8	1 × 17
	= −8 15	17

Sin (360 − A) = −8/17
Cos (360 − A) = 15/17
Tan (360 − A) = −8/15

Now let's address the big issue which I had left at the beginning. The above examples will let you find the value of any trigonometric angle without remembering the formulas as discussed in the beginning.

Example:– If Sin60 = √3/2, find the value of Sin 300, Cos 300 and Tan 300

Solution:– We Know that Sin A = Perpendicular / Hypotenuse

Hence, for Sin 60 the missing triplet will be $2^2 - (\sqrt{3})^2 = 1$. If you don't want to do this then you can use the figure method discussed above to find the value of Cos 60 which will let you find the value of the other missing triplet. Let's see how we can find the values using triplets.

Arrange the triplet accordingly.

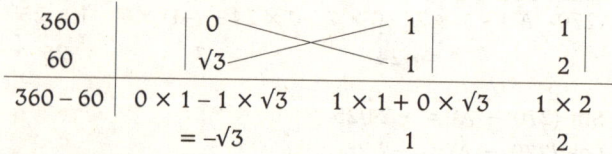

360	0	1	1
60	√3	1	2
360 – 60	0 × 1 – 1 × √3	1 × 1 + 0 × √3	1 × 2
	= –√3	1	2

Sin 300 = –√3/2
Cos 300 = 1/2
Tan 300= –√3/1

I do hope you have understood how easy it is to find the value of any angle for any trigonometric ratio. Let's do some practice to strengthen our concepts.

a) Sin 450   b) Sin 270   c) Cos 240   d) Tan 330
e) Sin 120   f) Cos 150   g) Sin 720   h) Sec 450

Computing Trigonometric Ratio of Twice the Angle (2A)

As discussed above, the triplet for angle A is – a, b and c. On extending the result for twice the angle i.e. 2A, we can see that the triplets for the angle 2A are **2ab, $b^2 - a^2$ and c^2**.

Take an example. We have Sin A = 3/5

Here a = 3 and c = 5, so obviously b = 4

Now make the triplet for twice the angle, i.e. for 2A.

The triplets are–	**2ab**	$b^2 - a^2$	c^2
	$2 \times 3 \times 4$	$4^2 - 3^2$	5^2
	24	7	25

Hence,

Tan 2A = 1st value / 2nd value = 24 / 7.

Example:– If Cos A = 9 / 41, find Cos 2A

Solution:– First find the triplet for angle A.

Cos A = 2nd value / 3rd value = b / c

Hence, the missing triplet a = 40.

So we have, a = 40, b = 9 and c = 41.

Now the triplets for 2A are–	**2ab**	$b^2 - a^2$	c^2
	$2 \times 40 \times 9$	$40^2 - 9^2$	41^2
	720	1519	1681

So,

Cos2A = 2nd value / 3rd value = 1519 /1681

Computing Trigonometric Relation for Thrice the Angle (3 A)

We have so far seen the triplets for angle A and 2A - let's extend it for 3A to find the value of Sin 3A, Cos 3A and Tan 3A.

The triplet for 3A are– $3ac^2 - 4a^3$ $4b^3 - 3bc^2$ **and** c^3

Let us take an example to understand the modus operandi more clearly.

Example:– If Tan A = 7/ 24 find Sin 3A and Cos 3A?

Solution:– The triplet for angle A –

Tan A = 7/24 = 1st value / 2nd value

Hence the missing part of the triplet = 25 = 3rd value, i.e. a = 7, b = 24 and c = 25

Let us find the values of triplet for angle 3A.

The triplets are–

$3ac^2 - 4a^3$	$4b^3 - 3bc^2$	c^3
$3 \times 7 \times 25^2 - 4 \times 7^3$	$4 \times 24^3 - 3 \times 24 \times 25^2$	25^3
11753	10296	15625

(For square and cube of a number refer to the *The Essentials of Vedic Mathematics.*)

Hence Sin 3A = 1st value/ 3rd value = 11753 / 15625
Cos 3A = 2nd value/ 3rd value = 10296 / 15625

Computing Trigonometric Relation for Half the Angle (A/2)

If the triplets for the angle A are a b and c then the triplets for A/2 are:

a   b + c   and $\sqrt{(b + c)^2 + a^2}$

Example:– If Sin A = 12/13 find the value of Tan A/2.

Solution:– We have Sin A = 1st value / 3rd value

Here, a = 12   c = 13 therefore from the triplets table b = 5.

Now find the triplet for A/2.

a	b + c	and	$\sqrt{(b + c)^2 + a^2}$
12	5 + 13		$\sqrt{18^2 + 12^2}$
12	18		$\sqrt{468}$
12	18		$6\sqrt{13}$

Hence Tan A/2 = 1st value/ 2nd value = 12/ 6 $\sqrt{13}$ = 2 /$\sqrt{13}$

I do hope the method discussed here will help you understand the concepts of trigonometry without taking any help from your friends, and once you have enough practice of the method you will get mastery over it, and begin to enjoy the technique and do all calculations in your mind irrespective of how difficult the solution looks.

14

Conversion Made Easy

This chapter is a mix of several different things commonly used by students in competitive examinations. The conversion of one unit into different is taught at primary levels but still we don't use it properly. Here we shall learn the conversion of–

1. Temperature
2. Kilometre/hour to metre/second and vice versa
3. Kilometre to mile
4. Pounds to kilograms
5. Adding time

Temperature

Conversion of Celsius degree to Fahrenheit and Fahrenheit to Celsius is simple if you learn the following formula

$°F = 9/5\ C + 32$
$°C = (F - 32) \times 5/9$

The conversion of temperature using the above formula involves a lot of calculation and is boring but there is no other formula. So you can ask me whether there is any other shortcut method which will help us to change the temperature scale if not to the exact value then close to that. The answer is a big YES.

- In order to change Fahrenheit to Celsius, subtract 32 degrees and then halve the remainder.

- To change Celsius to Fahrenheit, double the value and add 30.

Example:– Change 72°F to °C

Solution:– Let's do it first using the shortcut method and then using the conventional formula.

Shortcut Method:–   Subtract 32 = 72 – 30 = 40
Halve the result = 40 ÷ 2 = 20

Using Formula:– °C = (F – 32) × 5/ 9
= (72 – 32) × 5/9
= (40 × 5) ÷ 9 = 22.2

You can see that there is a slight variation in both the results but as told earlier, you can easily make an estimation of the result using the shortcut method.

Example:– Change 64°F to °C

Solution:– Let's do it first using the shortcut method and then using the formula.

Shortcut Method:–   Subtract 32 = 64 – 32 = 32
Halve the result = 32 ÷ 2 = 16

Using Formula:– °C = (F – 32) × 5/ 9
= (64 – 32) × 5/9
= (32 × 5) ÷ 9 = 17.7

Example:– Change 12°C to °F

Solution:– For changing Celsius into Fahrenheit we need to change our calculation. First using the shortcut method and then using the formula:

Shortcut Method:–   Double the value = 12 × 2 = 24
Add 30 = 24 + 30 = 54

Using Formula:– °F = 9/5 C + 32

$$= 9/5 \times 12 + 32$$
$$= \underline{108} + 32$$
$$\ \ 5$$
$$= 21.6 + 32 = 53.6$$

Example:– Change 25°C to °F

Solution:– For changing Celsius into Fahrenheit we need to change our calculation. First using the shortcut method and then using the formula:

Shortcut Method:–   Double the value = 25 × 2 = 50
Add 30 = 50 + 30 = 80

Using Formula:– °F = 9/5 C + 32
$$= 9/5 \times 25 + 32$$
$$= 45 + 32$$
$$= 77$$

This is pretty close to the exact value which will serve our purpose of estimation.

Kilometre/hour to Metre/second

To change km/h to m/s multiply the result by 5/18.
 To change m/s to km/h multiply the value by 18/5.

Example:– Change 72 km/h to m/s

Solution:– Multiply 72 by 5/18 = $\dfrac{72 \times 5}{18}$ = 20 m/s

Example:– Change 64 km/h to m/s

Solution:– Multiply 64 by 5/18 = $\dfrac{64 \times 5}{18}$ = 17.7 m/s

Example:– Change 15 m/s into Km/h

Solution:– Multiply 15 by 18/5 = $\dfrac{15 \times 18}{5}$ = 54 Km/h

Example:– Change 45 m/s into Km/h

Solution:– Multiply 45 by 18/5 = $\frac{45 \times 18}{5}$ = 162 Km/h

Kilometre to Mile

To convert kilometre to mile divide the value by 8 and multiply the result obtained by 5

Example:– Convert 80 kms into miles

Solution:– Divide 80 by 8 = 80/8 = 10
Multiply by 5 = 10 × 5 = 50 miles

Example:– Convert 24 kms into miles

Solution:– Divide 24 by 8 = 24/8 = 3
Multiply by 5 = 3 × 5 = 15 miles

Kilograms to Pounds

- To change kilograms to pounds multiply the result by 2.2. This can be simplified if you multiply the kilogram by 2 and divide the answer by ten. Now add both the results.
- To change pounds to kilograms divide the result by 2.2

Example:– Convert 65 kgs into pounds

Solution:– 65 × 2.2 = 65 × 0.2 × 11 = 13 × 11 = 143 pounds
This can be done in three steps in the following way:
Multiply the result by 2 = 65 × 2 = 130
Divide the value by 10 = 130 ÷ 10 = 13
Add the two results = 130 + 13 = 143 pounds

Example:– Change 86 kgs into pounds

Solution:– Multiply 86 by 0.2 = 17.2
Multiply again by 11 = 17.2 × 11 = 189.2 pounds

Adding Time

You don't have to worry about adding twice in hours and minutes. Add them simply like you do in addition. Once you have your answer, add 40 to it and you have the magical figure.

Example:– Add 4 hours 34 minutes and 5 hours 57 minutes.

Solution:– Add 434 and 557
$$434 + 557 = 991$$
$$\text{Add 40 to it} = 991 + 40 = 1031$$

Hence, 4 hours 34 minutes + 5 hours 57 minutes = 10 hours 31 minutes

Example:– Add 6 hours 24 minutes and 2 hours 57 minutes.

Solution:– Add 624 and 257
$$624 + 257 = 881$$
$$\text{Add 40 to it} = 881 + 40 = 921$$

Hence, 6 hours 24 minutes + 2 hours 57 minutes = 9 hours 21 minutes

Hope you have enjoyed the magic tricks and would love to use them. Here are a few practice problems for you.

a) Convert into m/s: i) 54 km/h   ii) 45 km/h   iii) 35 km/h
b) Convert into km/h: i) 24 m/s   ii) 65 m/s   iii) 48 m/s
c) Convert into pounds: i) 76 kg   ii) 87 kg   iii) 66 kg

Bibliography

- Bill Handley, *Speed Mathematics*, John Wiley and Sons, Inc., New York (2003).
- Gerard W. Kelly, *Shortcut Math*, Dover Publications, New York (1969).
- Edward Stoddard, *Speed Mathematics Simplified*, Dover Publications, New York (1994).
- Kjartan Poskitt, *Everyday Math Tricks for Grown-ups*, Reader's Digest Association, New York (2011).
- S. Bhushan and B.S. Gupta, *Calculation without Tears*, Ocean Publications, Delhi (2010).
- Rajesh Kumar Thakur, *Mathematical Magic*, Rising Publishers, Delhi (2008).
- Arthur Benjamin/Michael Shermer, *Secret of Mental Math*, Three Rivers Press, New York (2006).
- Arthur Benjamin and Michael Shermer, *Think Like a Maths Genius*, Rupa Publications (2006).
- Edward H. Julius, *Rapid Math Tricks and Tips: 30 Days to Number*, John Wiley and Sons, New York (1992).
- Shakuntala Devi, *Figuring: The Joy of Numbers*, Orient Paperbacks, Delhi (2006).
- Ann Cutler and Rudolph McShane, *The Trachtenberg Speed System of Basic Mathematics*, Souvenir Press, UK (2011).